Praise for *Trap Tales*

"*Trap Tales* is a triumph! The book reveals the 7 traps that can turn life's journey into an obstacle course. With clear examples and calls to actions, David Covey and Stephan Mardyks give you tools to escape and avoid these harmful traps. Read this book, apply its wisdom, and live your best life."

—Ken Blanchard, bestselling coauthor of *The New One Minute Manager* and *Leading At a Higher Level*

"Wow! What a tremendous book. I found myself enraptured by the story. Covey and Mardyks created characters that the reader comes to truly care about and whose stories they want to follow. That, along with very insightful content, creative analogies and relevant examples kept me deeply engaged throughout. I genuinely loved it."

—Jim Loehr, cofounder of the Human Performance Institute, renowned performance psychologist, bestselling author

"Covey and Mardyks are a dynamic duo! They've broken free from the standard approach to bring us a novel, hopeful book—one that shows that we can change the trajectory of our lives. If you feel trapped by circumstance or stuck in old patterns of thinking, read *Trap Tales* and breakthrough."

—Liz Wiseman, bestselling author of *Multipliers* and *Rookie Smarts*

"Anyone interested in learning how to avoid the basic pitfalls of life will enjoy the engrossing read that *Trap Tales* delivers. Covey and Mardyks eye opening story of life imparts invaluable wisdom and is an amazing guide for people of all ages."

—Stedman Graham, bestselling author, speaker and entrepreneur

"Few in the world of personal and organizational development have a more comprehensive view of all the field has to offer. I highly recommend a careful reading and application of the accumulated wisdom Covey and Mardyks have to offer for both spotting and liberating ourselves from life's most subtle and pernicious traps."

—Joseph Grenny, cofounder of VitalSmarts and bestselling coauthor of *Crucial Conversations*

"Freedom in not only a mental and physical construct . . . it is a core human need. Traps catch us and hold us prisoner in unhealthy repetitive cycles. *Trap Tales* imparts invaluable wisdom that can truly set you free. This book is your key to that freedom."

—Brian Tracy, bestselling author of *The Psychology of Selling* and *Eat That Frog*!

"Wouldn't it be great to be born with X-ray vision? Imagine being able to see what's up ahead or around the next corner, aware of every obstacle in your path. This entertaining book is an amazing guide that enables the reader to do just that."

—Bonnie St. John, bestselling author of *Live Your Joy* and coauthor of *Micro-Resilience*

"David and Stephan have identified the most common things that trip us up in our lives and work, and they've supplied a set of practical techniques for directing our focus to transcend them. An easily digestible manual for getting sticky things unstuck!"

—David Allen, bestselling author of *Getting Things Done*

"I always believed wisdom could only be acquired through hard-earned experience, but *Trap Tales* proves me wrong. It is rich with advice you can immediately act on. Read this book and you'll learn specific strategies for avoiding the most common mistakes while capturing life's greatest moments."

—Andrew Sobel, bestselling author of *Clients for Life* and *Power Questions*

"This book addresses a far more important topic than success in business. Instead, it is a remarkable treatise on overall success in life. It is chock-full of practical advice on how to avoid or extricate yourself from the many traps into which people fall. It is a powerful wake-up call to anyone who is innocently walking into a trap. It also sets some warning flares around traps by vividly and viscerally describing their consequences."

—Jack Zenger, CEO of Zenger Folkman and co-author of the bestselling *The Extraordinary Leader*

"To start thinking about our challenges as traps offers all of us a new and compelling framework that transforms our current predicaments. This book is brimming with insights and approaches that will surprise and amaze you."

—Don Yaeger, nine-time *New York Times* bestselling author

"As story analysts, we appreciate the authors' fine-tuned attention to the story—giving us rich characters and compelling struggles that deliver powerful concepts. David and Stephan have raised the bar for story-based business books."

—Wendy Gourley and Amy White, directors of Second Sight Studio

TRAP TALES

OUTSMARTING THE 7 HIDDEN OBSTACLES TO SUCCESS

David M. R. Covey
Stephan M. Mardyks

WILEY

Printed in the United States of America

10 9 8 7 6 5 4 3 2 1

Contents

Foreword by Stephen M. R. Covey

You might think it's automatic to trust your brother because you're related to him, but that's not always the case in families. Fortunately, it is the case in ours!

I've known David his whole life and I'm grateful to be able to share this foreword to a tremendous book that has the potential to shift your thinking and impact the rest of your life. Not only am I related to David, but I've also worked with him in a variety of capacities, and I truly trust him. Not only because of our shared parentage. Not only because he has sterling character. Yes, character is essential to credibility but so is competence, and David offers *towering competence*—his unique insight, capabilities, perspective, and expertise. Those who have worked with and for him routinely describe him as the best leader they've ever encountered. Plus, he is such fun to be around! David is very real, cares profoundly for people, and makes everything so enjoyable.

Stephan is a French Texan with a deep soul and strong propensity for Smart Trust. I lovingly call him the International Man of Mystery because he has traveled so much, seen so much, and quietly done so much to improve people and organizations all around the world. He is David's equal in character and competence, and he has a curator's instinct for what's distinctive and insightful. Let me share a story that illustrates Stephan's can-do beliefs and strong abilities to trust wisely. When launching *The Speed of Trust,* I met with Stephan to explore having his company distribute our program internationally. Stephan listened closely, asked a couple of questions, and extended his hand, saying, "This will be big. Let's do this. I trust you. We'll figure it out." That was it! No long drawn-out negotiations and endless cycles of back-and-forth legal agreements. (Yes, we did later work out the details of a business decision that was founded on this short, 30-minute meeting.) My experience with Stephan powerfully confirms the principles that are expressed in my work regarding trust.

Together David and Stephan are a great team and have been for years. This book is a product of their complementary strengths. They are both "make it happen" people. Both consistently deliver results. Both have an entrepreneurial edge, great business instincts, inspiring leadership skills, and the ability to naturally extend trust. They believe in people and balance a propensity to trust with good thinking and analysis, resulting in wise judgment. It doesn't surprise me they would write a story to illustrate the principles that will help you succeed in your work and life—both men value fewer words, greater action, and learning fast and forward.

Now let me tell you about the marvelous read you're about to experience.

To avoid a trap you need to see it. You will vicariously experience the awakening of the main character, Alex, as he comes to realize through the coaching of a family friend, Victoria, that he has foolishly been caught in what David and Stephan have termed "The 7 Hidden Obstacles to Success." The impact in Alex's world is not only felt in his career—it affects him even more in his personal and family life. These 7 Traps are seductive, enticing, and not always obvious. Fortunately, Alex chooses to extricate himself from these traps—but the purpose of the story isn't to experience the relief of Alex's change—it's to shine a light on how these common 7 Traps may enslave each of us.

You may not have fallen into all of these traps, but unaware, you—or someone you care about—may wander into them and be imprisoned, harmed, or limited. At a minimum, you or they will be knocked off the path of achieving what you could accomplish and become. Like Alex in this story, you will see that it takes time to escape from these traps, but it is possible to make your way out.

For each of the 7 Traps they've identified, David and Stephan reveal a corresponding "epiphany breakthrough." For followers of our father Stephen R. Covey's work, it's another term for what he called a "paradigm shift"—and I know that paradigms can shift. These epiphanies are not just moments of clarity—they can transform every succeeding moment. Our father used to reference Thomas Kuhn's book, *The Structure of Scientific Revolutions*, and how most breakthroughs in science were truly "break-withs"—that is, they were a courageous break with traditional ways of thinking. And that's precisely what David and Stephan have done with these traps: rather than lean on current conventional wisdom, they offer eureka-like approaches to help you see—and choose—a new way forward so you can both get out of the traps and avoid them in the future.

You might wonder where these 7 Traps and their corresponding epiphanies come from. What if you could read hundreds of books on improving human and organizational performance? What if you could talk in depth with their authors? What if you could participate in their programs? What if you could interview hundreds of independent business owners in dozens of countries about the challenges they face in growing their businesses and impacting their communities and nations? Stephan and David have done just that. They are partners in a business, SMCOV, that helps authors and training companies take and scale their ideas and approaches (through both books and programs) to global audiences. This remarkable experience, combined with past senior leadership roles at FranklinCovey, DOOR International, and Raytheon Learning, provides a very practical approach to the vital challenges that beset so many of us today.

You are in good hands with these two. They know what they're talking about. The 7 Traps are real and will capture the unaware and foolish. It reminds me of my work with trust and how people don't realize its importance until they experience it themselves. I believe you'll find that this story, and the traps it illustrates, will truly affect your behavior, your joy, and thereby the outcome of your career and life.

Perhaps the greatest gift of this book is hope. If, like the protagonist of this story, you find yourself in one or more of these traps you may wish you had never fallen into it, it's important to realize that you *can* get out. And stay out. And help the people you care about do the same. In the process of doing so, you will earn the dividend of increased self-confidence—greater self-trust—enabling you to become and give to others a truly great gift: a person they can trust.

Stephen M. R. Covey
Cofounder and Global Practice Leader of
FranklinCovey's Speed of Trust Practice
Author of *The Speed of Trust* and
former CEO of Covey Leadership Center

TRAP TALES

PART

1 | Alex's Story

The Story Begins

An irrepressible smile spread across Alex's face as he lightly tapped the accelerator of his brand-new luxury convertible. The shiny black car leapt smoothly from 0 to 60 mph with a burst of power that sent his head reeling.

"Now this is really living," he mused as he merged into the fast lane on the interstate. "Nothing quite like the smell of new leather."

The Southern California sun blazed, and the wind whipped through his hair as he put the top down with one click of a button. Catching a glimpse of himself in the rearview mirror, he was struck by his reflection. Looking good. He felt younger than he had in a long time.

The drive home ended all too soon. In no time at all he pulled his sparkling new acquisition to a stop in front of his home in an upscale Los Angeles neighborhood. Wouldn't his wife and kids be thrilled with his flashy new purchase! He couldn't wait to see their reaction when he boasted about his latest coup—a deal that had been too good to refuse. One minute he had been on a test drive, the next he was talking about a down payment . . . before he knew what had happened he was driving his new car off the lot!

Alex bounded up the front steps and through the front door with the energy of a man half his age.

"Kim, kids, get out here, there's something I've got to show you!" he exclaimed.

His two teenagers, lounging in the front room, barely raised their heads to acknowledge their father. Kim looked up from the desk where she was seated, poring over the family's finances, with an inquiring look on her face.

"What's all the excitement about?" she asked.

"Come on, you've got to see this," he said. He grabbed her hand and nearly dragged her out the front door.

He felt her jerk to a stop as her eyes settled on the gleaming new car parked in front of their house. Her face registered disbelief mixed with despair. This was not the response he'd been hoping for.

"What is it? What's wrong?" he asked anxiously.

Kim had sunk down to sit on their front steps, looking like she might collapse at any moment. "Alex, what have you done? Where is your car? Where did this convertible come from?" she gasped.

"I got the best deal ever! It was a no-brainer! We had the money, and putting $8,000 cash as a down payment gave me the lowest interest rate possible."

"You can't be serious. You can't be *serious*!"

"Kim, honestly. You're overreacting," Alex responded.

"Overreacting?" Kim cried incredulously. "That $8,000 was set aside for our trip to Hawaii! That was our entire year's savings! And you just up and decide to blow it all in one go . . . on something we didn't agree upon? Out of the blue? No discussion? Unbelievable!"

"But Chaz said we wouldn't see a deal like this again. I had to move fast," Alex defended.

"Please! Chaz? I don't ever want to hear that name again," Kim exploded.

Chaz, Alex's friend and coworker, was always encouraging Alex to live life the way he lived it himself. That meant extravagantly, at least according to Kim. She had reminded Alex all too often that Chaz's bachelor lifestyle had nothing in common with theirs. As far as Kim was concerned, Chaz was a bad influence and a bad friend. The expensive golf trips to beach resort locations were one thing, but to blow their stash of $8,000 on a down payment for a new luxury convertible was going too far. What about the sedan Alex had been driving? It was barely three years old.

"Babe, don't worry! Seriously. I've got another credit card that will pay for our Hawaii trip—it's all taken care of."

"But I don't want to add any more damn credit card debt to what we already owe! We're up to our eyeballs in debt, Alex!" Kim raised her voice angrily. "You take that car to the dealership tomorrow and get our money back. You don't need a new car and we don't need any more debt."

"I can't do it. It's already paid for. And I got an awesome trade-in price for my old set of wheels. Chaz said we couldn't pass up a deal like this. He used to sell luxury cars, Kim. He knows these things. C'mon, let's go for a ride. You'll feel better after you see how great it handles!"

"I'm not speaking to you anymore, not tonight. You either take back that car or I'm not going to Hawaii next week."

"Kim, honestly. It's done. Don't be insane. Of course you're coming to Hawaii."

"I'm serious, Alex. You have a decision to make." Kim stormed back inside the house, slamming the door behind her.

Alex and Kim slept in separate rooms that night. The next morning, Alex drove the shiny black convertible to work. Chaz was eagerly waiting for him in the parking lot.

"You are looking sharp in that car, my friend! How about letting me borrow it for my date this weekend?"

Alex laughed. "And who's your girlfriend this week? Is it still Jasmine?"

"Jasmine?" Chaz said with a hint of disgust. "I broke up with her two weeks ago. I'm dating Darci now." Chaz passed his phone to Alex to show a selfie he'd taken with his new girlfriend on the beach.

"Nice photo. But I don't think so, Chaz. What if she spills a drink on the leather seats?" Alex joked.

"Good point," Chaz laughed. "Come on, let's go make some sales."

Alex had little time to dwell on whether Kim would follow through on her threat. His day was packed with meetings and calls, one right after another. At the end of the workday Chaz and a few other coworkers were going to go out for drinks and watch the game together. Alex didn't want to seem antisocial—besides, he wasn't really looking forward to seeing Kim right then. He decided to tag along, just for a few minutes.

Before he knew it, it was nearly nine o'clock. Alex couldn't believe it had gotten so late. He excused himself from the group. Only one missed call from Kim. Maybe she wouldn't be so angry after all. He wondered what she had made him for dinner.

Alex knew he was going to be in trouble when he got back, yet he couldn't help but smile as he considered the drive ahead. Sliding behind the leather steering wheel, he gripped it firmly as he pulled out of the parking lot and onto the road. "This feels so right. Kim will get over it," he told himself. "It's just a matter of time."

Soon he was lost in the joy of handling the sleek convertible as it responded to the slightest touch, as if he and the car were made for each other. He resisted the urge to take the long way home—it wouldn't do to upset Kim further. As Alex wheeled into the driveway and opened the garage door, he noticed her car was missing. She must be out running an errand, he thought.

Alex walked into the kitchen where his son Michael was doing math homework at the table. "Hey Mikey, where's Mom?"

Michael kept his head buried deep in his textbook. "You really stepped in it this time, Dad." Alex's heart sank. Where was she? He climbed the stairs to their room and found a note lying on the bed.

Alex tore open the envelope.

Alex, I can't believe how self-serving and inconsiderate you've been. I'm leaving for San Francisco. Remember that job I was offered last month? I'm going to go check it out. The position still hasn't been filled, and they were thrilled to hear I might be interested. It's nice to feel like someone cares about what I have to say. It might make sense for us to be apart while we sort things out. Let's talk when you get back from Hawaii. I've already told the kids about my plan. Please take good care of them while I'm gone. —Kim.

Alex immediately tried to call her, but she didn't pick up. He texted her, but she didn't respond. He couldn't believe this was happening. How could she do this to him? Who was going to look after the kids? Her sense of timing was unbelievable! Alex felt overwhelmed by the injustice of it all. He fell back on the bed, unable to wrap his head around what she'd done. He glared at the ceiling until hot angry tears blurred his vision. How had everything gone so wrong? Was this the straw that finally broke the camel's back?

* * *

A week later, Alex found himself alone, standing on the balcony of his hotel room on the 34th floor, overlooking the Pacific Ocean. He stared blankly at the turquoise Hawaiian surf, watching it foam up on the shore as the tide rolled in. His kids had already changed into their swimsuits and were headed for the beach, ready to soak up every moment of Spring Break. Laura was relieved to be free from her Advanced Placement classes, and even Michael, who enjoyed his studies, couldn't leave Junior High behind fast enough. They had wanted to have fun with their friends over the break, but who could pass up a week in Hawaii, even if they had to hang out with their old man?

It had been more than three years since Alex's last vacation. He'd been promising his kids he would take them to Hawaii when his life slowed down. The problem was that life never seemed to slow down. In fact, it seemed to be speeding up.

He wished he could stop time, stay in this beautiful scene, and forget the world he had left behind in California. The future now felt uncertain, and instead of his usual confidence, he felt insecure and alone. He was unsure how things would play out with his wife, and he almost didn't want to know.

Alex shrugged his shoulders to release the tension of these burdens. That morning, looking in the bathroom mirror, he'd noticed how his thinning hair was turning gray. But the sight and sound of the pounding surf was having a calming effect on him. He began to reflect on key events that had transpired in his life.

Alex and Kim had met their freshman year in college. They were always bumping into each other around campus. They were good friends for two years before their relationship turned romantic and they became a couple. They married soon after graduation. At first they didn't have a lot of money, but they didn't mind. They were young, smart, ambitious, and, most importantly, in love.

They had come to this very hotel for their honeymoon. Alex remembered how happy they had been, remembered the feeling that their whole lives lay stretched out before them and anything was possible. Nothing else mattered as long as they could face life together. How lovingly Kim had looked at him then, and how much fun they had together. Alex smiled as he remembered the night Kim dared him to go skinny-dipping in the ocean, and how she had grabbed his swimsuit from the beach and ran back up to the hotel with it. They made sandcastle villages, rode bikes through the tropical forest, and snorkeled with the most colorful fish he had ever seen. It had been unforgettable.

Once Alex got his first job, the income was great. But Alex reveled in it and spent every cent he made, enjoying every luxury he could. He didn't save a dime.

Alex's decision to get his master's degree only added to their debt, but with an advanced degree came better paying jobs and more opportunities. Just as Kim started to advance in her own career, she became pregnant with Laura. Three years later Michael came along. A few years later Kim went back to her work as an accountant, but even with her income it never seemed like there was enough. A mortgage, car payments, household expenses, and credit card debt started piling up higher each year.

Despite Kim's efforts, Alex never managed to establish any habits around saving and investment. Each time he got a bonus or a job promotion, the extra money seemed to evaporate. Alex and Kim's expenses were now growing out of proportion to their income. He began charging frequently and liberally on his credit cards.

From the beginning, Alex justified and defended his spending. Luxuries became necessities. He needed his country club membership so he could golf with his business associates like Chaz. To keep up with his coworkers, he had to take the same sort of expensive vacations and cruises. He loved high-end watches and the latest technology gadgets. To Alex, who'd been brought up in this lifestyle, these expenses weren't extravagant. But 20 years into their marriage, Alex and Kim had zero savings, no retirement money in the bank, and a pile of debt.

When Alex's company was going through financial difficulties during the recession, he was laid off without any warning. Alex had always been a top performer, so he assumed he would not be susceptible to occasional downsizing or restructuring. He never imagined that his company would become disrupted, obsolete, irrelevant, or that he could lose his high-paying job.

Alex remembered that time all too well. His mind flashed back seven years.

He had arrived home from work much earlier than usual. He normally got home around 6:00 or 6:30, but never as early as 3:30 in the afternoon. Kim, who had been working from home that day, was in the laundry room folding a huge pile of clothes from several wash loads.

"Hey, honey," Kim smiled. "What are you doing home so early?"

"I just got laid off," he blurted out in a state of shock.

"What?" She dropped the shirt she was folding. "You're kidding, right? You're one of the star executives at that company. How could they possibly lay you off?"

"I know. I know. It's not about me. Apparently the company ran out of cash, so the whole thing went bust. We all lost our jobs, just like that," Alex said, bewildered.

Kim seemed lost in thought. "Did anyone see this coming?" she asked.

"I certainly didn't. I'm sure my boss must have known," Alex said.

"I mean, I knew company cash was tight, but to completely run out of money? It's ridiculous," he fumed. "How can you run a business and not have a plan for getting more cash? It's downright irresponsible!"

The company Alex worked for had been around for 35 years and in its heyday had generated almost $500 million in annual revenue. Despite its respectable revenue stream for a privately held business, it had always managed its expenses poorly. In its most recent year, the company had generated around $350 million in revenue but had not adjusted expenses or downsized the number of employees accordingly.

"So what do we do now?" Kim asked, a hint of fear in her voice.

"I guess I start looking for a new job," Alex responded dejectedly.

"It's pretty brutal right now. Have you seen how many jobs we've lost as a country in the last six months? Who knows how long the job hunt could take? I guess we could cut back on eating out so often, and we could cancel that expensive country club membership." Kim began pacing as she calculated other ways to save.

"Kim, Kim," Alex said, reaching for her hands. "Don't worry about it. No need to do anything extreme. We'll figure it out." He could see in her face that she wanted to believe him. But there was a twinge of something else there, too.

Alex snapped out of his reverie. They had figured it out, but it took a lot longer than Alex had imagined. For eight months, he searched and searched for a new job before finally landing with his current employer six years ago. He probably would have kept looking for something better if Kim hadn't insisted that he swallow his pride about the pay package. He had been a successful sales executive for seven years. Why weren't companies willing to pay for his valuable skill set?

Alex's unbridled confidence and cheery optimism took a big hit after he was laid off. What bothered him most, now that he was earning only 60 percent of his previous salary, was the pressure to put the brakes on his comfortable lifestyle. He couldn't stand the thought of resigning his country club membership, or abstaining from luxury vacations and the newest technology. That would be asking too much. Sure, *too much* debt was no good, but throughout his life he'd always managed to juggle *some* debt.

Lately he'd been so stressed out about his work—and then there was the fight with Kim—that he hadn't faced the enormity of his situation. He started to add up all the debt he'd accumulated. The family had $50,000 in credit card debt, a $278,000 mortgage, and two car payments totaling $900 a month. Laura would be in college in 18 months. How was he going to pay for that? She had her sights set on a university in New York City that several of her high school friends were planning to attend. But the out-of-state tuition was astronomical, and without any savings, Alex and Kim clearly couldn't afford it. He didn't know how they could afford in-state tuition, for that matter. Why hadn't he planned ahead and put away some money for Laura's education?

Alex couldn't believe how unprepared he was. How could he have been so foolish and shortsighted? And what would he do about paying down the debt?

He contemplated, just for a moment, the idea of raiding Michael's bank account. His son was very secretive about how much he had saved, but at only 14 years old, Alex was sure there was at least $15,000 in his account. Michael was a saver who rarely spent anything. He also had a knack for capitalizing on money-making opportunities. Since Michael was 10 years old he had made money for himself by mowing the neighbors' lawns and selling off the gadgets his family no longer used.

Alex pushed the desperate thought aside. He was on vacation, for goodness' sake, and he didn't want to focus any more on his financial woes. This was finally his time to recharge, refresh, and recover from all the hard work and difficulties he'd faced over the past few years. He threw on his swimsuit and made his way out to the beach to take in the salty air and goof around a little with his kids.

Nearly two hours later, the sun was setting, and after playing so hard everybody was hungry. Alex wanted to take his kids to one of his favorite places on Oahu—Roy's Restaurant. Wet, sandy, and barefoot, the three of them returned to their room to change for dinner.

As Alex walked back into his room he spotted an envelope on the nightstand with two chocolates on top. He opened the envelope, which contained a beautiful card detailing the schedule for the vow renewal ceremony he and Kim had planned together when they set up the trip.

Just then, his phone vibrated. It was a text message from Kim. She had accepted the job in San Francisco.

What? Was this for real? Alex couldn't believe she would choose to move away from the kids. He always thought the kids would keep her in Los Angeles. How could she do this to him? How could this be happening? Tears of frustration filled his eyes.

He didn't have much time to dwell on it, because just then, Laura started pounding on his door.

"Dad, what's taking so long? I'm starving!"

"One second, I'll be right out," Alex called back weakly. He splashed some water on his face and tried to pull himself together before he faced the kids.

* * *

Roy's food and service was better than he had remembered—even his kids were impressed. As they finished their entrees, Alex's phone buzzed—an email from Chaz. It looked like the deal they had been working on for the past six months was going south. Alex sighed and began to tap out a response.

His attention was diverted by a familiar voice. "Alex? Alex, is that you?"

Alex looked up from his phone to see an old friend walking over to their table.

"Alex, it's been ages! What fun to run into you after all this time, how are you?"

"Victoria? What are the odds! I'm here on vacation. These are my kids, Laura and Michael." He gestured to them as he introduced everyone to each other. "Do you guys remember the stories about me growing up with my best friend Bobby? This is his mother Victoria. She's practically a mother to me too."

Michael leaned over toward Laura and whispered, "Wait, is Bobby the one who . . . ." Laura nodded at him knowingly.

Victoria winked at them. "But no one had better start calling me Grandma! It's wonderful to meet both of you. So where's Kim?" she asked, looking around. "It's about time I met her."

Alex winced. He hadn't yet thought of what to say in a situation like this.

"Well, um, we're actually working through a few issues right now."

"Oh, I'm sorry. I didn't mean to intrude," Victoria said, a little embarrassed.

"Oh it's all right, no worries," Alex stammered. He was saved by the waitress, who had just arrived at the table with dessert menus and was waiting expectantly.

"Well I don't want to hold you up," said Victoria, "But I would love to catch up with you while you're here in my corner of paradise. Here's my card, Alex. Please call if you have some free time." She leaned over to the kids, "Make sure to ask your dad about the Great Egg Fiasco. Has he told you about that one yet?"

"Nooooo," they said in unison, turning to Alex with expectant grins on their faces. Alex was flushing red, and called after her, "Not cool, Victoria!" She turned around and gave them another wink as she waved goodbye.

Alex and the kids finished dessert and headed back to the car. He couldn't believe that he'd run into Victoria after all this time. They had exchanged birthday cards over the years, but Alex hadn't seen Victoria in person since the funeral. But he didn't want to think about that right now.

Victoria had a certain way with people that made them want to be around her. It was easy to be drawn into her presence, with her ready smile and the sense of peace and contentment she exuded. She was always so warm and encouraging, and rarely seemed out of sorts. Nothing ever seemed to faze her. Meanwhile, Alex felt like he was barely holding it together. He decided he would give her a call the next day. Maybe some of that optimism would rub off on him.

Trapology

After a good night's sleep, Alex felt more refreshed and relaxed than he had been in a long time. Sure, his life and finances were in disarray, but something about the warm Hawaiian air made him feel more ready to tackle his problems today. He pulled out Victoria's card and gave her a call while his kids were at the pool.

Victoria invited him for lunch at her beach house, a 20-minute jog from Alex's hotel. He ran along the ocean's edge and before long he saw her waving at him from the beach ahead. They walked past the back fence to a porch overlooking the water, where she suggested they eat their lunch. The rhythmic sound of the crashing waves was soothing. He closed his eyes to let the sound sink in while Victoria went into the house to fix the drinks.

Being with Victoria brought back a flood of childhood memories. When their families lived in the same neighborhood in Los Angeles, Victoria and Rob's only child, Bobby, had been Alex's best friend. The two were inseparable. They played football in the fall, hot tubbed endlessly in the winter, ran sprints in the spring, and surfed in the summer. They formed the best beach volleyball team that the world had ever seen (or so they believed). People used to think they were brothers because they were always together.

Like most teenage boys, they talked about girls and sports. But their relationship was deeper than that. They shared their life goals, dreams, and aspirations, as well as their worries, fears, and doubts about the future. They sucked the marrow out of everything life had to offer two teenage boys. Their world was full of endless possibilities for a bright future.

Then, in a blink of an eye, everything changed. At age 17, Bobby was diagnosed with terminal cancer. He was given six months to live. It seemed too impossible to believe. Alex was stunned and refused to accept the diagnosis. Rob and Victoria pursued every medical treatment available in an attempt to prolong their son's life. But their efforts only served to prolong Bobby's misery. Little by little, he wasted away.

Alex remembered the last time he saw Bobby before he died. They drove to their favorite beach, where they'd made so many great memories, but this time it was different. There were no volleyballs, no flying Frisbees or footballs, and no slipping through the surf. Bobby's body was frail and weak. He barely had enough energy to stand up outside the car for a moment, even with Alex bracing him. It tore Alex apart to see how every movement caused his friend so much pain. Several days later, Victoria called him—Bobby was gone.

The passing of his best friend altered Alex in profound ways. He promised to live life for both himself and Bobby. All the experiences Bobby had wanted to have, Alex would pursue on his friend's behalf. He vowed that he would never take life for granted. He realized it could all be taken away at any given moment. Alex's endless activity and boundless energy, his drive to do things now, now, now frequently annoyed Kim. But she hadn't understood that Alex was living life for two people.

Victoria's footsteps brought him back to the present. "So Alex," she said, as she settled back into her chair. "What have I missed? I can't believe your children are so big! It makes me feel old."

There was something about the sound of the waves and the warmth in her voice that made Alex feel like he could let his guard down and share his problems with her. He knew Victoria would listen without judgment. He started to speak and the words came tumbling out in a rush to be heard and understood. He laid it all out—the car, the split with Kim, the debt, the nagging feeling of disillusionment that he couldn't seem to shake.

Victoria was a good listener. She didn't jump in and try to relate. She never interrupted except to ask clarifying questions. She just listened intently to what he had to say.

"Honestly Victoria, I just don't get it. I don't know how I ended up in this state of affairs. I thought I was going somewhere. I thought I had the perfect family. But now I look around and it's all falling apart." Alex finished, staring down at the sun-bleached wooden table.

Victoria nodded thoughtfully, searching his face, as if trying to determine something. Alex looked up and met her gaze, a dull pain and sense of despair in his eyes.

Suddenly Victoria stood up and motioned to Alex, "Follow me, I want to show you something." She turned around and went back inside the house, moving surprisingly fast for a woman her age. Alex scrambled out of his chair, trying to catch up.

Victoria's house had a strong smell of lavender and incense—a little too strong for Alex's taste. The soft sounds of a sitar played from somewhere in the background. As Alex looked around he saw the incense burning in a handmade ceramic pot in the corner next to her yoga mat. The kitchen counter was loaded with fresh fruits and vegetables in one corner, close to several pots of fresh herbs. A book titled *The Green Smoothie Bible* was open next to the blender. Since when had Victoria become such a hippie?

"Over here!" Victoria called out. Alex realized her voice came from beyond the open doorway, which was partially covered by strings of beads decorated with small elephants and bells. The bells jangled softly as he pushed past the curtain to follow her voice. Victoria stood in front of a beautiful red and black marble chessboard set majestically on a bamboo bistro table. Alex looked confused for a moment, then a light of recognition spread across his face.

"Tell me you haven't forgotten what this is," Victoria teased. Inspired by his mother, Bobby had learned to play chess when he was a little boy. Alex had been drawn into the game through Bobby, though he was never quite as good as his best friend. Sometimes Victoria would coach them, teaching them new moves to try out on each other. It made his heart hurt to see that chessboard. But he also found it somehow comforting, like a link to the past, or like coming home after a long time away.

"Of course I haven't, how could I?" Alex responded. "Tell me that you haven't forgotten who was the last to win!"

"Ha! As I remember, that was the only time, and it was because I was feeling bad for you. Selective memory, I see."

"Wow, it really has been a long time. This is the same board, right? I don't think I've played chess even once since then."

"Well I'll have to go easy on you then, won't I?" Victoria teased.

"So you're still pretty good, eh Victoria?" Alex countered.

Smirking, Victoria replied, "Pretty good? We both know I am way past pretty good. Come on now, Alex."

Victoria sat down at the table and invited Alex to sit across from her. Her tone turned a little more serious. "The truth is, I've become much better over time, but I used to lose a lot before I learned how to see things from the right perspective.

"Most of my losses in chess were caused by traps, traps I couldn't see because I didn't know how to look for them," Victoria said. "In chess, the term *trap* refers to a move intended to tempt the opponent to play a losing move and get stuck. If you can spot the traps in advance, there's no problem. If you can't, you will most likely lose the game.

"Traps, by definition, are not easy to detect, especially in the opening stage of the game. You can learn about traps the hard way, through trial and error. But it is better to learn from someone who already knows how to spot and escape them. Learning just a few simple tactics can save a player from disaster."

Alex nodded, listening intently.

Victoria continued, "Great chess players are masters at setting up traps and experts at avoiding them. Some traps in chess are so deadly that they are given names. Ever heard of the Monticelli Trap or the Blackburne-Shilling Gambit? I didn't think so. That's because traps are sneaky little devils until you study up and learn how to see them coming."

"Is there a Victoria trap?" teased Alex.

"Not yet, but maybe one day! I like to think more about escaping from traps than creating them. Here's the thing: studying how to spot, avoid, or get out of traps will give you a key tactical advantage, not only in chess, but in life as well," Victoria smiled.

"Alex, I'm going to give you a new perspective on life. Up to this point, you've viewed your challenges as just *problems*. Instead, I want you to start viewing challenges as traps."

"Traps?" asked Alex.

"Traps," Victoria confirmed. "What if we could learn to spot the traps of life, just as I learned to spot the traps in chess? What if we could learn the steps to pull ourselves out of the traps we're already stuck in? I've become almost obsessed with the idea. Rob teases me—he calls it *trapology*, or the study of traps. I'm no professor, but I actually quite like that name."

"So if you study trapology—that must make you a trapologist!"

"You could say that. And I'd like to make you a trapologist, too, if you'd care to learn."

"Only if we get to wear cool hats like Indiana Jones," joked Alex.

He was having fun now, but couldn't deny that he was intrigued. He wasn't sure if what Victoria had to say would actually help—it was probably just going to be some hippie mumbo-jumbo—but he was enjoying himself and felt willing to hear her out.

"Not until you're as advanced as I am, Alex. Be patient, my young grasshopper," Victoria responded with a sly smile. "True trapologists understand traps—how to spot them, how to avoid them, and how to pull themselves out of any they don't manage to avoid. Like experienced chess masters, trapologists learn to think many moves ahead."

Alex was staring at his phone. It had buzzed moments earlier and he had instinctively pulled it out. It was an update on the basketball game happening that day. The Lakers had gone up by three points—nice!

He suddenly felt Victoria staring at him. He looked up sheepishly and put his phone back in his pocket.

"As I was saying . . . traps are traps because they surprise you. They catch you off guard and before you realize what has happened, you are stuck. Have you ever seen quicksand before?" Victoria asked.

"Not in person, but I've seen it in movies like *The Princess Bride*," Alex replied. That movie had been a favorite of his and Kim's, and thinking of it took him back to happier times.

"Okay, good, so you know what I am talking about," Victoria responded, bringing Alex back to the present. "Like quicksand, traps are easy to step into, but are hard to get out of. The more you struggle and flail around, the deeper you seem to sink. Yet if you know what to do and follow the right steps, it is quite possible to escape quicksand. In fact, it's easier than you might think. And if you learn the telltale signs, it's possible to spot quicksand and avoid stepping into it in the first place."

She continued, "I once attended a presentation where Jack Welch, the renowned CEO of General Electric, described this 'ability to see around corners' as one of the key attributes of great leaders."

"If we could identify the traps that most of us face in our lives and learn the strategy and tactics to avoid them, how valuable would that be? Can you imagine if we could spot traps before they take us off course?"

Alex was a little skeptical. "Sure, that would be amazing if it were really possible. But nobody can see into the future."

"Of course—yes, you're absolutely right. But we can study the past. And if there is one thing we know about the past, it's that history tends to repeat itself. I'm not saying you should pull out a crystal ball, I'm simply suggesting that you pay closer attention to the world around you."

"I have to say, I was half expecting you to have one! It would fit right in with the rest of your decor," Alex teased.

Victoria narrowed her eyes. "You better watch it, or I might be adding that cocky head of yours to my collection!" she laughed.

"Okay, okay," Alex threw his hands in the air. "Shouldn't have said anything . . . touchy subject."

"But seriously, Alex. This is important. Many people say that experience is the best teacher in life. Unfortunately, it's also the hardest teacher—and the slowest. Too often, we learn about the harsh realities and pitfalls of life firsthand, and it's not much fun. You see—traps in life, like in chess, are easy to fall into but hard to get out of.

"What if we could learn from the experience of others, rather than having to experience it for ourselves? What if we could identify the markers on the path toward problems?"

Victoria paused. Alex watched her, waiting expectantly.

"Have you ever seen a father or a mother live a sports career they personally never experienced through their son's or daughter's own sporting experience? They are living vicariously through their kids. It's as if they were on that football field or basketball court themselves."

Alex nodded knowingly. Just at the moment his phone buzzed again—the game! But Victoria's look warned him not to pull out his phone again.

"What I am suggesting is this—when we learn of the traps that people around us have fallen into, we should really study what forces are at play. We can live vicariously through their experience and try to understand exactly how they got trapped, why they can't seem to escape, or if they do, how they managed it. If we do this right, we can avoid the pitfalls—the pain and the misery of making the same mistakes. Most people would give their right arm to do it over again."

"I don't know if I would give my right arm, but I might give up my left pinkie!" Alex chimed in.

Victoria laughed. "Let's keep your pinkie intact. At least until the next comment you make about my home decor."

Leaning back on his chair, Alex smiled. "All right Victoria, you've got me. I'm in! I'm ready to become a trapologist. But I have to insist that we get the hats."

"I'll think about it," replied Victoria with a grin.

They were silent for a moment listening to the sound of the sitar—now accompanied by a soothing, chanting voice—as it played against the background of surf hitting sand.

"You know," Victoria admitted, looking at the ground. "It was so hard when we lost Bobby. I think about him every day."

A lump rose in Alex's throat at the thought of his friend. He didn't know what to say.

"I thought we could fight his cancer and beat it. We got the best doctors and medical care on the planet to care for him . . ." she trailed off.

"They did their best. And at that point I don't know if anything more could really have been done for him. I don't hold any hard feelings in my heart. But when the medical system couldn't heal my son, it got me thinking—could there have been any other way? Was there anything else we could have done?" Victoria looked around the room, gesturing. "That's probably what got me started with all this. I realized that the conventional way of doing things, the way everyone encouraged me to act, didn't always hold the answers."

Their eyes met, and Alex nodded his head solemnly.

"I think there's wisdom in looking outside the box, learning to think for yourself and not just taking life as it comes at you, wave of crisis after wave of crisis, with momentary lulls in between. We need to learn to navigate intelligently so we aren't dragged helplessly under the riptides life brings our way. We each get to write our own story, be the author of our own destiny.

"Don't be a victim of your circumstance, Alex. You find yourself in a rough spot right now. I could have allowed Bobby's cancer to defeat me. Instead, it has opened up a world of possibility where each new day has potential for growth and learning. I can play at this game of life with wisdom and compassion. And if I can help others like you find a better way, it somehow turns my own loss into a victory of sorts."

She continued, "Why do you think so many people fall into the same traps over and over again? How can they see their friends and family fall into them, and then follow right along? Once they realize they are trapped, why can they never seem to get unstuck?"

Alex shrugged his shoulders.

"It's because they are following a conventional approach that may contain a strain of truth, but can never be enough. We can't keep doing the same things and expect different results. We need new thinking to get us to a new place. To truly avoid and escape the traps in our lives we need to look for the unconventional, and sometimes the counter-intuitive. I'm talking about breakthroughs, not incremental improvements. Breakthroughs only occur when you have a break 'with' the standard approach."

"Makes sense," Alex said, nodding his head.

"A lot of the traps we fall into today are not new—many of them are as old as time," Victoria continued. You can read about them in the most revered books of scripture, the most ancient texts. But what's different today is how the modern world has amplified these traps—making them more alluring, seductive, and sticky than ever before."

She pointed at the chessboard. "It's like we went from playing against kindergartners to playing against Garry Kasparov!" Alex couldn't quite place the name, but he nodded as if he knew.

"We need to be more aware if we want to identify the traps of the modern world, and more creative in the approaches we use to escape them, more than we ever were in the past.

"Alex, let me tell you about something I've been working on for a long time—a framework for how we can think about life's traps that will help you wrap your brain around it and see its application in your life."

"Okay, I'm listening."

"I haven't shared this with many people," Victoria confessed, "so I hope you don't mind being my guinea pig. I think having a framework can be very useful, because it helps us get a sense of our current state in a systematic way. It's impossible to move to our *desired* state (where we want to be) when we aren't aware of our *current* state. Does that make sense?"

"Makes sense," Alex confirmed.

"The core message of the Traps Framework is *hope*—the belief that humans can change the trajectory of their lives through wise choices and course corrections. This hope is essential."

Alex felt something stir inside him. Just yesterday he'd been feeling like there was nothing he could really do to fix the mess he was in.

As if reading his mind, Victoria said, "I'll be honest with you, Alex, you're in a pretty tough spot. As far as I can tell, you are caught in a whole mess of traps. You know this better than anyone. But you're not the first person, nor will you be the last, to fall into these traps. I should know!" She laughed as she rubbed her shoulder. "There is a way out. You can't let that spark of hope within you fizzle."

Their gaze met and Alex nodded with a thoughtful look in his eyes. Despite all the jokes, Victoria's message was becoming real for him.

Victoria continued. "With each trap we explore together, I'd like to help you learn to move from the pain you are feeling now to a state where you've escaped the trap and are able to thrive. There are four steps along the way, which I call the Four-Phase Progression: It begins with *pain*—feeling the awful reality of the trap; which triggers *recognition*—the realization that you are stuck in a trap; once you implement and stick with your strategy to get out of the trap, you know *success;* at which point you are free to progress, prosper, and *thrive* beyond the trap."

She paused to study Alex for a moment. His expression was concentrated—brow furrowed with lips pressed tightly together. He spoke slowly, "But . . . how am I even supposed to get through that process? How do I know what is and isn't really a trap?"

"I'm glad you asked," Victoria responded gently. "I've noticed that most traps have a few telling characteristics. As I've said, traps are like quicksand. Once we've stepped in quicksand, it's difficult to get free. We step into this quicksand, or trap, because we are unknowingly seduced, lured in by the promise of a quick-fix solution or by some temporary pleasure. Most traps cause short-term-itis, the thinking that the pleasure we get now is worth the pain we'll experience later."

"Sounds strangely familiar." Alex tried to force a smile.

"Hey, don't beat yourself up. Remember that you're not the first one to be caught in quicksand. Traps are, you guessed it—meant to trap us! They lie along life's path, disguised as if by leaves and moss. They appear innocent because we aren't equipped with the tools to see them for what they really are—seductive, deceptive, sticky, and limiting. Some of the conventional approaches out there may have some positive effects in the short run, but the traps we're faced with require nonconventional solutions to get us free of them for good. When we're deeply hurt, we don't need a Band-Aid—we need a cure. I like to call it an *epiphany breakthrough*."

Alex raised his eyebrows at the phrase.

"Yes, I know it sounds a little strange. But remember earlier, when I said that trapologists must look past conventional thinking to find unconventional wisdom? The unconventional wisdom is the epiphany, which leads to a breakthrough in behavior. Hence, *epiphany breakthrough*."

"Okay, I can roll with that," Alex nodded.

"Good, because you don't have a choice," Victoria teased. "By the way, I have something for you."

She pulled a thin red book out of her bag.

"As an official trapologist—okay, trapologist in training—there is a lot you'll need to remember. I'm giving you this journal so you can write down any notes or insights along the way."

"Wow, thanks Victoria," Alex said taking the journal in hand.

Just then a clock chimed right behind his head. He jumped in alarm.

"Easy there, Alex," Victoria laughed. "That's just a reminder about my yoga class. It's starting soon." She stood up and stretched her arms toward the sky. "I hate to cut our conversation short; I know you're really interested." She paused and looked at him intently once more.

He gave her two thumbs up and a cheesy grin.

"Good," she chuckled. "Good. Then come back tomorrow! I'd like to share with you an observation I've made—and a trap I see you've fallen into."

"What!" exclaimed Alex, half joking and half concerned. "I've already fallen into a trap? But you just made me a trapologist! I'm not supposed to fall into traps."

"A future trapologist," Victoria corrected. "Before you can learn to spot the traps coming your way, you must first get out of the traps you've already fallen into."

"Traps *plural*? More than one?" Alex stepped down the weathered stairs and back onto the beach.

Victoria had already turned back toward the house, "See you at breakfast!"

PART
2 | Traps 1–3

Trap 1: The Relationship Trap

The next morning, Alex left his teenagers sleeping and headed to Victoria's place, eagerly anticipating what she had to say. Was she going to offer the same advice as the marriage counselor that Kim had insisted she and Alex meet with last year? He hoped she would provide a fresh perspective.

She could certainly provide a fresh breakfast. Alex devoured the veggie omelet Victoria set in front of him, but he wasn't so sure about the bright green smoothie that came with it. Victoria had almost finished her own, and Alex wondered if he could avoid drinking his without her noticing.

"I'm so happy to be with you again, Alex. It reminds me of the good times we've had together." Her voice was cheerful, but Alex saw sadness belying her expression. "What I'd like to share with you this morning will give you a new perspective, a new way to think about your problems."

"Okay, I'm listening!" said Alex.

Victoria polished off the last of her smoothie. "Do I have a green moustache?"

"Yes, you do," Alex replied.

"Good! Call me Yoda."

Alex laughed. "I guess that makes me young Skywalker then? I'm good with that. As long as I don't have to carry you around everywhere in a backpack."

"No promises!" Victoria replied. "But seriously Alex, I've been thinking about some of the challenges in your marriage, and I want to talk with you about something I call the Relationship Trap. I've observed a pattern that traps both you and Kim. And actually, I've seen this pattern trap a lot of people. In fact, the relationship trap applies to anyone in a relationship, whether you are married or partners or otherwise. It applies whether you have children or not."

Alex swallowed and didn't say anything. This wasn't what he wanted to get into—it felt a little too raw. For an instant he regretted telling Victoria anything about his marriage at all. Alex worried that she was about to lecture him, just like that marriage counselor had done when he and Kim had gone for help. Reluctantly he asked, "So what's the pattern?"

"Well, it's a pattern that two people fall into when they are married but live as if they are single," Victoria replied. "In other words, they become married singles."

"Married singles?" asked Alex. Her response surprised him—this was new.

"Married singles means you live together but your lives are not integrated," she explained. "You operate as if you are living by yourself. When two people come into a marriage they bring two very different value systems, two ways of thinking about the way things should be. For example, take Kim and yourself as it relates to finances. You were raised in a well-to-do family while Kim grew up middle class. Is that right?"

"Yeah, you're right, but that's normal enough," quipped Alex.

"True," she agreed, "but most couples fail to realize the significant differences that exist, and thus they fail to establish a plan for how they will operate in their marriage. They unknowingly set a pattern for disagreements and contention. You've shared how you and Kim have fought over your finances from the beginning of your marriage to the present."

"That's right, Kim's such a tightwad," Alex muttered.

Victoria raised her eyebrows. "And why do you think she is that way?"

Alex muttered, "Probably because she was raised that way."

"And what way is that?" Victoria responded.

"Well, her mom's family wasn't very wealthy, but her dad's family used to have money until Kim's grandfather squandered their fortune," said Alex.

"So her parents probably had a difficult time recovering from that."

"Well yeah, they were shell-shocked. I guess I would be as well if that happened to my parents," Alex confessed.

"Your family is quite the opposite, don't you think?"

For the first time, Alex considered how each of their upbringings had colored their relationship. It's not that he was oblivious to the differences, but he had never pondered the implications until now. Kim's family had enough money to satisfy their needs, but they were otherwise extremely conservative in their spending. The story of her grandfather's negative investment venture was passed down to Kim and her siblings with the message that money was hard earned and easily lost. But money was always available to Alex growing up.

"Sure, I guess so. We've always had money, so we've never had to worry. Well, until now." Alex looked down, embarrassed.

"I believe that when couples operate as married singles they do so for three reasons. You want to hear what they are?" she said cheerily, seeking to lighten the mood.

Alex nodded.

Superior Upbringing

"Okay, the first reason is that they believe that their upbringing is superior to that of their spouse. They think that the way things were done in their childhood home is the right way to operate. Anything that runs counter to their experience is seen as different, weird, or just plain wrong. This applies to both the big and small things.

"The big things include how we raise our children, manage our finances, and share the responsibilities of the household," Victoria explained. "Small things could be anything that annoys us—how we squeeze toothpaste, organize our kitchen, arrange our furniture. You see? We make all of these judgments unconsciously, and become annoyed at the differences in our spouse or partner." Victoria cleared her throat. "I'm guessing you can relate to this?"

Alex shamefully shifted his gaze to the floor, "Unfortunately, the differences between Kim and me run very deep."

They sat in silence. Alex became lost in thought. Where had they gone wrong? How had he and Kim become disconnected in so many areas of their relationship? From finances to child rearing, they could never seem to get on the same page. Lately, their differing child-rearing philosophies had become a constant source of contention.

Alex's philosophy reflected how he had been raised—lots of flexibility and very little discipline or structure. He and his siblings never had to do any chores or yard work. All of the household duties fell upon his mother. The cooking, laundry, cleaning, trash, carpools, groceries—and whatever else—was left up to her.

Kim's experience was drastically different. Both her parents worked, so the chores were doled out between her and her younger brother. Her father was very involved in helping with the kids and around the house. The family followed a strict schedule for waking up and bedtime, and privileges were lost if she or her brother acted up or neglected their responsibilities.

When their own children came along, Alex and Kim's problems increased. Alex's upbringing and parenting style was manifested in Laura's behavior. When Kim complained about having to cook dinner without help every night, Alex and Laura simply went out to a nearby restaurant. Michael, more sensitive to his mother's feelings, would then make a simple meal for the two of them.

Even at school, the children reflected their parents' attitudes. Laura frequently missed class, always with the justification that she knew the material and would ace the test. Laura was bright, and despite her checkered attendance, she usually finished each term with good grades. Michael took after Kim. He was studious, reliable, and detail oriented. He turned in his homework on time, saved whatever money he earned, and never missed a day of soccer practice no matter how he was feeling.

Victoria interrupted Alex's stream of thought. "Have you and Kim ever taken the time to iron out your differences?" she asked.

"Honestly, not really. When we got married, I just expected our life to be the same as it had been for me as a kid. It probably sounds stupid to you, but I just assumed that Kim would do everything as well as work professionally. My family was pretty traditional that way. I mean, I don't see anything wrong with that way of life. I suggested Kim hire a housecleaner once a week, but she couldn't justify the expense."

"How do you think Kim feels about all this?"

"I don't know. It was hard when the kids came, even before she went back to work. She would get mad at me for not helping out more. I'd step in the door after working all day, and before I knew it she was hounding me to do the dishes. It just didn't seem fair to me, but she was probably thinking the same thing about me after spending all day with the kids." Alex felt a pang of regret. He thought of how selfish and unhelpful he'd been throughout their marriage.

The Mindset Shift to "We"

Victoria thought for a moment. "You and Bobby played football in high school together, right?"

"That and track."

"Okay, so other than the relay races in track, what's the biggest difference between the two sports?"

"Well, football is a team sport, whereas track is an individual sport," Alex ventured.

"Right," Victoria confirmed. "Today, too many couples are running track instead of playing football. They haven't made the transition in their marriage from an individual sport to a team sport, so to speak. You not only see this sports analogy in marriages, but also in businesses, governments, and "populace of entire countries.""

"I love sports analogies," Alex replied, "Kim hates them though. She rolls her eyes every time I use one."

"Noted. I won't use sports analogies around Kim. But that point leads us to the second reason I think couples operate like singles. They never shift their mindset from *me* to *we*," Victoria explained.

"When we shift from thinking only about ourselves, to including concern for our partner, we abandon our individual practices for the benefit of the team. Most couples don't spend enough time thinking like a team in their marriage."

Alex agreed. "At least in my case, you're definitely right about that."

You Change First

"The final reason why couples fall into this trap of selfishness, and have a hard time getting out of it, is that they wait for their spouse to change first. But you don't have this problem right, Alex?" Victoria winked.

Alex smiled sheepishly.

"Changing our behavior patterns is very difficult. Some people would rather die than change. This is seen in health care all the time—today's biggest health problems stem from overeating, drinking too much alcohol, not exercising enough, too much stress, and smoking—all of which we have some power to change. Most people would prefer to continue their lifestyle than make drastic changes in favor of their health. In fact, I just heard about a study that looked at people with severe heart diseases who had undergone bypass surgery—and just two years after the operation 90 percent of them had not changed their lifestyle.[1]

"When we wait for our spouse or partner to change first, we are often in for a long wait. The lack of movement in one partner makes the other partner feel justified in not changing either. But when our partner attempts to change, our conscience is pricked to reciprocate in kind.

"The best way to encourage change in your partner is to change first yourself. Have you experienced this in your own life?" Victoria asked.

"To be honest, Victoria, I haven't. I've built my whole life around the *I'll change if you change first* mentality. So I can't say I've seen the benefits from this approach. But I'm ready to give it a go."

"Glad to hear it."

Conventional Approach

"Alex, the conventional approach to marital differences is to agree to disagree and find other areas where we are more compatible. This approach acknowledges that we can't change others, and suggests that since we all come from different backgrounds and perspectives, we just need to accept those differences. However, if we can't create a mutual perspective on important issues, then we are likely to have a superficial marriage at best. When the difficulties and storms descend upon us, as they inevitably will, that relationship will not be able to stand, just as you have witnessed."

Epiphany Breakthrough

"Based on what you've told me," Victoria said, "I believe that your differing philosophies regarding money and unwillingness to come to an agreement about how it would be used has greatly contributed to your separation."

"Yeah," Alex admitted. "I guess it's just easier to blame Kim than to admit that I might have played a part in all of this, too."

"You must realize that neither of you were wrong in how you were raised to think about finances. Your upbringing was just drastically different."

"Yeah, well . . ." Alex massaged the back of his neck with his hand. "It takes two to tango."

"The mistake you have made, and the mistake that most couples make, is not getting on the same page and making a plan for how you are going to operate as a family. There are three main issues every married couple must agree upon: First, how will you manage your finances. Second, if you have kids, how will you raise them? And third, how will your household duties be divided and managed? For example, will each of you work professionally, or will one partner be primarily responsible for the care of the children?

"Most couples fall in this trap when they don't discuss their differences in order to come up with solutions. They don't take time to visualize and write their own family story. It's easier to just repeat what you've seen modeled. As a result, you end up having two people in a marriage who operate with two different mindsets—like singles. Have you and Kim had conversations about these important issues in your marriage?"

"I wouldn't quite call them conversations. We've certainly fought about them though." Alex grimaced.

"As we've been talking, I've started to realize why we've had so many disconnects," he continued. "We just couldn't be more opposite. We haven't managed to find common ground to build upon." Alex spoke softly, looking down at his hands.

"Alex, operating as a single is one of the most common traps I see in married life. You aren't alone in this. I believe this kind of counsel should be given to every newly married couple by requirement before they get married," Victoria said to console him.

"Yeah, this would have been helpful years ago."

"It's not too late to have the conversation. Is this something you'd be willing to talk with Kim about? It's not too late to write a new story for your family," Victoria prodded him gently.

"I think so," Alex responded. "I have a lot of thinking to do first. I haven't made many concessions in our marriage, and I need to spend some time considering the compromises I'm willing to make and follow through on."

"That's great, Alex. But it's not so much about compromise as it is about creating a shared vision, a shared story: the story of you, as a couple. What are you working toward together? What amazing things will you share? What memories will you build? This is the fun part! The modern world offers more opportunities to us today than ever before.

"Once you answer these questions, the next thing to discuss together is how will you live that story in your day-to-day life? What do each of you need to do? How will you share the load?

"The root problem for individuals operating as singles is not having a reason to change. Living life by your own standards and expectations is easy and comfortable. You don't have to integrate, adapt, or compromise. Though technically united, you can live out your own single story as you see fit," Victoria explained.

Alex realized that both he and Kim were living out their own separate stories. The passing of Bobby altered Alex's story. His response was to live life to the extreme. Kim, on the other hand, had seen her parents lose everything. Her response was to live life very cautiously and carefully.

Because they were playing out their scripts for their own separate stories, they weren't on the same page in their relationship. What united them? What brought them together? These questions deeply resonated with Alex. He realized that developing their own unified story was the key in transforming their relationship. They needed to decide on their goals, their dreams, and their aspirations for their relationship and family, and then agree upon a pathway to get there, together. He hoped it wasn't too late.

Victoria continued to explain her theory. "The primary reason we fall into the relationship trap is because we tend to resist adjusting our mindset from a *me* paradigm to a *we* paradigm. When we begin to look at our relationship as a team instead of as independent individuals, we can begin to address the issues contained in this powerful trap. We cannot address the relationship trap issues from the me (or individual) mindset. We can only address the relationship trap issues from the *we* (or team) mindset. The critical first step for change is *mindset*. All subsequent decisions emerge from that first step; without it we are unable to move forward. Got it?" Victoria queried.

"Got it," answered Alex.

Alex looked down at his notes.

Trap 1: The Relationship Trap

Why?

1. We believe our upbringing is superior to that of our partner's.
2. We fail to shift our mindset from *me* to *we*.
3. We are unwilling to change, or we only agree to change if our partner changes first.

Conventional Approach

Focus on things both partners agree upon, minimize or altogether ignore differences.

Epiphany Breakthrough

Create a shared vision for your relationship/marriage and agree upon a pathway to get there together.

Victoria checked her watch. It was approaching noon. Nearly three hours had passed since Alex had knocked on her door.

"Alex, my yoga class is starting in 15 minutes. Can we meet again in another two days?" Victoria asked as she slipped on her sandals and walked toward the door.

"Yes, please!" Alex replied. "But I feel like I'm imposing on your time. Are you sure it's not an inconvenience?"

"Not at all," said Victoria. "I'm glad for our time together; it's nice to have some company while Rob's out of town. I've really enjoyed reconnecting after all these years."

* * *

Alex arrived back at the hotel and was greeted by an all too familiar sight. Both of his kids were sitting there in the hotel room, in total silence, eyes glued to their phones. They barely looked up when he entered the room.

"Laura, Michael!" He got right up to their faces but they didn't look up. "Aloha! Guys, we're in *Hawaii*. What are you still doing on your phones? Let's get outside, go to the beach, do something fun!"

Laura waved her hand at him without looking up, "Dad, one sec. I've just got to watch this."

Michael joined in, "I've almost got to level 9. Give me a minute."

Alex rolled his eyes. He'd heard this story all too often.

When Laura finished catching up on social media she turned her attention to her father. "What about you, Dad? Why don't *you* go to the beach? You've just been hanging out with that Victoria lady this whole time. Is she holding the Great Egg Fiasco against you as blackmail?"

Alex couldn't believe that Victoria had mentioned the Great Egg Fiasco to his kids, even if in passing—that story was meant to have died out long, long ago. He and Bobby had plenty of escapades from their mischievous youth, but he wasn't about to let Laura know about them.

"She's actually a pretty awesome lady; I've been learning a lot from her," Alex said. He thought for a second. "You know, guys, my parents never told me anything about their lives. They tried to shield us from everything and believed there were things you just didn't talk about. But I wonder now if that was such a good idea. Maybe I could have avoided the mistakes I made if they had been more open with me."

Michael had just beaten level 8 and was looking up at him now with a strange expression on his face.

"It's been really hard not having your mother with us on this trip. This was where we came for our honeymoon, and this was where we were going to celebrate our anniversary."

"Gross, Dad, we don't need to hear about that," Laura moaned.

"I know, I know, I'm just saying it's hard not to have her here with us," Alex admitted.

Michael's face began to flush. He jumped in, "Well, it's your fault she's not here, Dad! All your fault! You always do this! If you didn't go and spend all the Hawaii money on that stupid car she *would* be here." Michael turned away so they couldn't see his eyes welling up with tears.

"Hey . . . Michael." Alex went over to Michael's bed to give him a hug, but Michael pulled away from him. Alex sat there for a second, thinking of what he could possibly say.

"Look, you might be right, Michael. But whoever is to blame, there is one thing that's for sure: Your mom and I have not been on the same page, not about this, and not about a lot of things." Alex exhaled, and then continued. "This is actually what Victoria and I talked about. She said that when two individuals come together and get married they often don't make the transition from *me* to *we* in their marriage."

"What do you mean?" Michael asked, wiping his eyes.

"Well, it's kind of similar to a soccer team." Alex saw he had his son's attention. "Have you ever been on a team where the players are out for themselves? Where each player is doing their own thing— going for their own goals and their own glory? And then there is the opposite—have you ever seen a group so integrated and coordinated that it seems like the members can read each other's minds?"

"I guess," Michael acknowledged.

"Well, marriage follows a similar pattern. When two individuals come together in a marriage, but they don't decide on how they are going to work together as a team, that is the equivalent of being a married single."

"If you say so," Michael shrugged.

"Let me give you another example from my job. Recently I promoted one of my star salespeople, James, to sales manager. James was great at selling, and I believed that if he could teach others his approach, his team could be as successful as he had been. But the problem was that James couldn't make the transition from being an individual performer to a team leader. Instead, he always insisted on being in the spotlight. He didn't realize that as a team leader, it was no longer about him—it was now about the success of the team as a whole. He couldn't make the transition from *me* to *we*. And as a result, I unfortunately had to move him back to his previous role as a salesperson."

"So which one of you is James in this situation?" Laura asked, a bit sarcastically.

Alex ignored her tone. "Well, probably both of us in our own way. Neither Mom nor I have really come together about anything. In fact, we have been polar opposites. I'm loose and carefree with my spending, while Mom is careful and disciplined. I'm also relaxed and hands-off in my parenting approach, while your mother is strict and hands-on."

"Yeah, Mom and you are like total opposites," Michael said. Alex had the feeling that this opinion didn't reflect so favorably on him.

"Kind of like me and you, M-dog," Laura chimed in, shooting her hair elastic at Michael's face. It barely missed. He threw a pillow back at her.

"But there is a reason we're both like that." Alex continued. "I'm behaving the way I was raised. My parents and siblings are not careful about money either."

"Well, why budget and be careful about money when you don't have to be?" observed Laura.

"Right! That had been my attitude for a long time, but now I'm in a place where I'm struggling to make ends meet. So, I need to examine and perhaps even change my philosophy.

"Another thing Mom and I see differently is our roles at home. Tell me this, guys—am I really as bad at helping around the house as Mom makes me out to be?"

The kids looked at each other as if the answer was obvious. "Dad," Laura said, "you're worse. I haven't seen you wash a dirty dish in years."

"Well at least I take care of the garbage—are any of you making sure it gets out on time?" Alex challenged. "I didn't think so. It's not like I don't do anything. When I was growing up my mom did *all* of the housework, garbage included."

"Grandma was a slave," Laura said.

"That's what your mother says. She reminded me every day when she came home from work that she is not my slave."

"Well, Dad," Michael hesitated, "It's true."

"I realized that my mother and yours have completely different circumstances. My mom didn't work outside of the home—she was a full-time mother and homemaker. Your mother, on the other hand, has worked full-time, except for the few years she was home when you were little," Alex said.

"Look, I've probably been a little insensitive to her situation," he continued. "I've also been too loose in my spending habits, especially since you little rugrats were born." Laura's lips curled in disgust at Alex's choice of words, but he ignored her.

"Don't take it all upon yourself, Dad," Michael jumped in. "You're not the only one who can't help buying everything you touch," he said, looking smugly at Laura.

"Whatever, Michael," Laura rejoined. "Like you're so perfect?"

"Now, now, let's just say you've been a good follower of my ways," Alex said, trying to lighten the mood.

"So does that make me the golden child?" said Michael.

"Oh, gimme a break," said Laura, rolling her eyes.

"Hey you two, be nice. I need your help. This split with Mom is helping me take a hard look at our relationship and how we interact as a family. I want you two to be a part of the solution. We can choose what our family life is like, how we treat each other, how much fun we have together. Just because we haven't figured it out in the past doesn't mean we can't going forward. Our history doesn't dictate our future unless we allow it to. We can write a new story for our family."

Laura looked at Michael skeptically. Michael shrugged.

"So, Dad, what are you asking for? I'm no playwright!" Laura said with reservation.

"I'm just asking you kids to think about it. Envision the kind of family life you would ideally like to have. What kind of activities and memories do you want to create together? How could we get more aligned with our spending habits so we are working toward a common goal as a family, instead of being divided? Just think it over while we are here on vacation, and we'll talk more about it when we get home."

"Enough talking, I want to go swimming!" Laura declared as she rolled off the couch and headed to change.

Alex laughed. This was the first time he'd ever had this kind of interaction with his kids, and he was impressed with their maturity. He realized that by admitting some of his own failures and shortcomings, his kids were able to do the same. He felt a renewed sense of hope— that united they could navigate their issues. He only wished Kim had been present to witness it.

Trap 2:
The Money Trap

Alex spent most of Tuesday relaxing with his kids at the beach. He marveled at how therapeutic the ocean was for his psyche. He had been stuck in the mode of *go go go* for so long that it felt refreshing to actually have a whole day dedicated to doing absolutely nothing.

The next morning, Alex woke up feeling refreshed after the best night's sleep he'd had in a long time. He went out for a run on the beach. He was amazed at his level of energy and felt ready for whatever Victoria had in store.

Alex knocked on the door of the beach house.

"You look five years younger than you did in the restaurant the other night," Victoria exclaimed.

"I feel renewed. I didn't realize how burned out I was," agreed Alex. "I've been looking forward to our conversation today."

"Well, the wait is over! Let's get started outside. Breakfast is on the porch."

Alex's run had made him hungrier than usual, and he downed his omelet in a couple of minutes. He pretended to sip on the smoothie Victoria had made—today it was a nauseating shade of greenish brown—but when she went inside to grab some napkins, he quickly tossed the contents of the glass into the bushes.

Victoria looked suspiciously at Alex's lack of smoothie moustache when she came back, but decided to let it go.

"Alex, do you have your Trap Journal?"

"Right here!" he said, holding up the red notebook.

"Great. Let's talk about your debt."

Alex leaned forward. This one he had seen coming, and he was ready for any ideas that could help him—he sure didn't have any.

"Debt is one of the most pernicious traps people fall prey to. They don't realize it as such, and therefore don't take the necessary precautions. They haven't been trained to recognize the warning signs."

"What warning signs?" asked Alex.

"They're part of the basic traits of traps, the ones we talked about the other day, remember? Seductive, deceptive, sticky, and limiting. Taking on debt is a classic example of all four."

Alex nodded, ready to get up to speed.

"Well then, from my experience on the subject—there are three primary reasons people fall into the debt trap." Victoria took a deep breath. "First, they have a condition I like to call 'money myopia.' They live in the moment, without thought for the future, and lack the self and family discipline to forgo unnecessary expenses, which incur debt. Second, they are caught in a cycle of competitive consumption, or trying to 'keep up with the Joneses.' And third, they're in denial—they don't believe worst-case scenarios apply to them, they only happen to other people."

"Hey, this is getting personal!" Alex said, taking mock-offense.

Money Myopia: Living in the Now

Victoria smiled playfully. "It seems that people are willing to do almost anything to get more money—except the main thing required, which is to exercise restraint and self-discipline when it comes to their spending habits. I say self-discipline because children will follow the habits and behaviors modeled by their parents. If the parents exhibit a carefree, live-in-the-moment attitude, their kids will most likely follow suit."

"I can relate to that," said Alex. "My daughter is just like me in that way."

"I sensed that when I met her the other night. You probably spoil her to death. She's daddy's little princess, right?"

Alex laughed, "It sounds like you've been talking with my wife."

"I haven't, I just have a knack for reading these things in people. Anyway," she continued, "if we don't have a plan for managing our money, we will go with the flow and allow the pleasurable and fun things of life to crowd out the strategic direction of our financial plan. Learning to live within our means after deliberately budgeting for savings, investments, education, and retirement requires discipline and resolve. If we are only living for today, we will never have the self-control and determination to make this happen.

"What makes this especially challenging to avoid is how easy it has become to get what we want by going into debt. Spending has become so seductive. We get a credit card preapproval in the mail. The credit card describes the benefits we'll get, the rewards we can earn, and the freedom we can attain through its use. Sure, there are some benefits that come with credit cards, but they certainly don't outweigh the devastating downside that comes if you get into crushing credit card debt. Credit card companies want you to become indebted and dependent. They don't want you to pay your balances off. They want you to pay only your minimum amount so that they can earn very high interest from your purchases and over-extensions. Does this sound familiar to you?"

"Embarrassingly familiar," said Alex. "What about the other two reasons?"

Competitive Consumption

"Okay, the second reason we fall into the deadly debt trap is our desire to keep up with those around us who seem to be happier and wealthier than we are. We get caught up in the acquisition of *stuff*. This mindset pervades the world we live in. We start to believe that the purpose of money is to acquire, so we acquire a lot of unnecessary stuff. We spend, spend, spend! I spent most of my younger life trying to keep up with others. It's a hard cycle to break. But in the last few years I've learned the vacuous nature of that approach," Victoria admitted.

"The problem with stuff," she continued, "is that it demands our attention. We have to protect our stuff, fix our stuff when it breaks down, and buy new stuff when it doesn't work anymore or goes out of style. Do you know what the word *entropy* means?" asked Victoria.

"Yeah, actually, I think I do. I learned it in one of my science classes in college," Alex said. "In physics, I think? It's the idea that everything in the universe eventually moves from order to chaos or disorder. Am I right?"

"That's it—the gradual decline into disorder. Think of your children's bedrooms."

The connection made Alex chuckle. "That's a *rapid* decline into disorder. I could live much easier with the gradual decline."

"Well, you get the point. It's the problem with all of the stuff we buy—from our homes, to our cars, to our appliances, to our toys, to our clothes. It all starts to unravel from the moment we move into our new house or drive that new car off the lot. But Alex, the bigger problem is that when we buy all that stuff with a mortgage or with a credit card, we are stuck in the quicksand of debt. And let's make no bones about it, it is quicksand."

"Ah, I can relate all too well to that." Alex shifted and looked down at his hands. "I've never thought about it in those terms, but the analogy is definitely accurate." He thought about how dependent he'd become on the income from his job because of his lifestyle.

"So, what is the third reason?" asked Alex.

Denial: Worst-Case Scenarios Don't Apply to Me

"The third reason we fall into the debt trap is because we believe in the status quo," Victoria continued. "Most of the time the status quo is a good thing for us. We bought our house at a certain price and in a couple of years it is going to be worth 20 to 30 percent more. Why? Because that is what houses do most of the time—they appreciate. That is, until they depreciate and we have a housing bubble crisis like we just experienced, and then suddenly you are underwater. You find you owe more on your house than you own."

"How did you know that about me?" said Alex.

"I just guessed it. You probably expected there would always be a safety net waiting for you," she continued. "You've worked hard—stayed committed to your company—believing that you had an endless runway of promotion, salary increases, and bonuses, right?"

"Hey, no one expects that they're going to be laid off," Alex defended.

"Alex, that's exactly why we fall into the debt trap. Because we fail to anticipate the unexpected, or we pretend we didn't see it coming. A new leader emerges and we fall out of favor. Our company gets acquired or fails to adapt to a new technology that revolutionizes the industry, and we—like our company—are caught flat-footed," Victoria replied.

"That's exactly what happened to me," Alex bemoaned.

"When we believe that the sun will always shine, our prospects will always be bright, and our earning power will be endless, we are ripe for the worst-case scenarios to mess up our lives. We need to regularly ask ourselves: How long will my present financial situation continue? What would happen if my income were cut in half or eliminated entirely? Would I have the means to service my debts and fixed expenses? We need to be prepared for the worst-case scenarios to play out in our lives. Have you ever thought about these things, Alex?"

"I mean, I try to," he said weakly, realizing how silly that sounded as it came out of his mouth.

Victoria thought about calling him out on that, but sensed that he already felt overwhelmed by all he had to change.

"Just remember this—debt is your deadly enemy; debt is quicksand. And one of the biggest problems in accumulating debt is the interest we pay on it.

"I'd like to share with you a quote about interest I like so much that I typed it up, framed it, and hung it on my wall. Come look at it," Victoria said as she stood and motioned for Alex to follow her.

As Alex stood up, he checked his phone for any messages. There was another email from Chaz titled "****URGENT****PLEASE RESPOND ASAP****." He couldn't help but open it, but he noticed Victoria waiting for him with a curious look on her face. He put the phone back in his pocket. Stupid phone wouldn't load the message out here anyway.

"This is it," Victoria said, pointing to a quote within a gold picture frame.

Alex began reading:

Interest never sleeps nor sickens nor dies; it never goes to the hospital; it works on Sunday and holidays; it never takes a vacation. . . . It is never laid off work nor discharged from employment; it never works on reduced hours. . . . It has no love, no sympathy; it is as hard and soulless as a granite cliff. Once in debt, interest is your companion every minute of the day and night; you cannot shun it or slip away from it; you cannot dismiss it; it yields neither to entreaties, demands, or orders; and whenever you get in its way or cross its course or fail to meet its demands, it crushes you.[1]

Alex sat in silence for a minute or so after reading the quote. He had never imagined interest in this way, but it described his situation perfectly. How did Victoria know him so well?

Victoria interrupted the silence, "Can you relate to this?"

"Every day of my life. It's scary, but it's so true," Alex admitted. "Why would you keep this quote hanging on your wall though?"

"Because, I've fallen prey to debt and the demands of interest in my life as well. You think you've got it bad? You have no idea the burden I once was under. Now, whenever I get the smallest temptation to slip back into debt or go on a spending spree, I read this quote and do otherwise."

Alex was impressed with Victoria's transparency, but was becoming depressed about his own situation.

Victoria saw his dejection. "Come on, Alex, buck up! You can't go back and change the past. It's done. But you can course-correct as you go forward. I see that you're in the right frame of mind now to start learning about the strategies and tactics that will help you get out of the debt trap and escape from the quicksand you've unwittingly fallen into," Victoria said with a smile, trying to cheer him up.

Conventional Approach

"My problem with most of the books I've read on debt—and I've read nearly everything out there—is that they advise a strategy that, more often than not, fails in its approach. Usually, that strategy is to budget," Victoria explained.

"And to be clear, Alex, I'm not suggesting you shouldn't try to adhere to a budget. It can be an important part of your financial plan. I am simply saying that in my experience, budgeting alone is not enough to help people escape debt. That's because budgeting requires willpower, and lots of it. And while people can exercise restraint in the short run, it is rarely successful in the long run. Similar to a New Year's resolution to lose 20 pounds by sticking to the latest diet plan, willpower begins with a lot of hype and fanfare, but it quickly fizzles out. That's why you see so many people fall into the debt trap over and over again. And what's worse, the more times they fall in, the more they become convinced that they can never escape."

Epiphany Breakthrough

Alex didn't look like he felt any better about his situation.

Victoria was quick to reassure him. "But here's the thing, Alex. They *can* escape. Some do escape. I'm living, breathing proof of that. Not so long ago, Rob and I were deeply ensnared in the debt trap, too. We were buying designer clothing, taking vacations in exotic locations, dining at expensive restaurants, and purchasing unnecessary and extravagant luxuries on our credit cards. But we didn't feel bad about our expenditures because we were receiving loads of airline and hotel points—and anticipating all of the money we'd save on our next vacation because of those points! Have you ever justified your spending like that?

"We knew we had to change our ways," Victoria continued. "But we didn't really know where to start. We tried budgeting for several months and failed miserably. We would occasionally make some progress, but then one of us would slip up and we would end up where we'd started.

"We needed an unconventional approach. Rob had been volunteering at the local recreation center, where he coached a basketball team of young teenagers. During scrimmages, he noticed that when he turned on the gym's scoreboard and started tracking who was winning, the boys tried a lot harder. However, when they just played against each other without tracking the score, they would soon stop going for all the rebounds, stop playing defense, and start taking lazy shots. Rob learned to always turn on the scoreboard when he needed the team to focus.

"One day, when we were discussing our finances when Rob proposed an idea: 'What if we were to apply the same scoreboard principle to our debt? We could keep track of progress and create our own scoreboard to show it.' Our debt wasn't really a competition, so we couldn't use a basketball scoreboard. But I had a different idea. We'd just returned from a trip to the Amazon. While we were there we saw many snakes, big snakes, monster snakes—creatures that Rob has a deep and abiding fear of. When he asked me how I thought we should track our debt, I remembered this and suggested, 'What if we used a snake?' Rob grimaced, but replied that as long as we didn't bring any real snakes into the house it wasn't such a bad idea.

"We bought a roll of butcher paper and began to draw and cut out the shape of the snake. It had a big head with a long body that began in the kitchen and extended into the family room. Each section of the paper snake had lines that represented $1,000 of debt. We had nearly $90,000 in credit card debt at that point. The paper snake was longer than the python snakes we saw in the Amazon. The plan was to totally eliminate all of our credit card debt as quickly as possible. As we made progress, we would cut off an increment of the snake's body.

"We were amazed at how the snake motivated us, and how quickly we eliminated all of our credit card debt—twice as fast as we had anticipated. We moved on to tackle our two car loans, and then the mortgage. We did all of this in fewer than five years!

"Inspired by the success we'd had in scoreboarding our debts, we decided to create a visible scoreboard for what we termed our 'Big 3 Strategic Financials.' These were:

1. Cash savings
2. Investments
3. Retirement funds

"Now that we had eliminated our debt, we began to take all the money we had once allocated to paying it down and used it instead to build wealth. This we did to fulfill our long-term goals and plans. We wanted to harness the power of compound interest, which Albert Einstein referred to as the 8th Wonder of the World. Before, interest had been working against us—creating more debt. Now we would get it working in our favor.

"To this purpose we created a luscious green paper tree with three main branches, each representing one of the three buckets of our financial plan. Instead of cutting, trashing, and burning this scoreboard, we would attach leaves to the branches of our tree, each representing a $1,000 contribution. The greener our tree became, the more growth we saw in our savings account.

"Because we were used to putting this money toward debt, it wasn't difficult to now channel it toward these three buckets. Each month we put $1,000 in savings, $1,000 in investments, and $1,000 in retirement funds. Over time, each of the branches became heavy with green leaves.

"We began to automate our monthly withdrawals—$3,000 a month dedicated to our three branches—to occur on payday, which was, for us, the first Friday of every month. In the beginning it felt very harsh, but once these funds were stripped from our accounts, we learned to live on the remainder of our paycheck for the rest of the month. Most people make the mistake of making these strategic investments last instead of first. The problem with that approach occurs when there's nothing left in your account by the end of the month. So, although your intentions may be good, you can't follow through on them. Financial strength and security depend on proactively establishing good habits.

"Alex, these positive habit patterns completely altered the financial trajectory of our lives in ways we couldn't possibly have imagined. We only wish we had done this from the start."

Alex nodded appreciatively.

"So what is the epiphany breakthrough regarding debt? The traditional approach suggests you need to be more disciplined, create and stick to a budget, and exercise restraint in the hard moments. And although this is true, it does not work the majority of the time for most people—at least not by itself. The unconventional solution is to create a scoreboard and make a game out of reversing debt and creating a flourishing savings plan."

Victoria, now finished, looked for Alex's reaction.

"Wow, that's amazing. I can't believe you were in so much debt!" said Alex. "And I thought I was the big spender."

"How do you think I paid for all my vintage home decor, Alex?" Victoria teased back.

Just then the clock went off again. It was noon. Three hours had flown by. Nothing about Alex's debt had changed, but Victoria's framing of his debt as a trap, and her ideas to use the paper snake and tree as tools to rebuild his finances were enormously energizing to him. He wondered if these strategies might even work at the office.

Victoria interrupted his train of thought. "Here's the main point I want to leave you with, Alex: Money can be your tool or your taskmaster. When people are deeply in debt, money becomes their master; their choices are limited, their options are reduced, and they find themselves living in bondage. When people allow money to work for them through the power of compound interest, their money is multiplied and unleashed. It gives them leverage.

"When we feel the pain of being lulled into debt's all-encompassing, suffocating grip, we can talk with others who are also in debt to learn from their insight and regret. When we make a game out of debt elimination, we can capture the interest and hearts of our family members so that they, too, will change their behaviors, uniting everyone involved in a common effort and goal.

"We need to be motivated and enthused by progress toward our strategic financial goals, such as our return on investments, our contributions to our children's educational funds, the growth of our retirement funds, and our savings and emergency back-up plan to compensate for loss of income and other potential disasters. Does that make sense to you, Alex?"

"Yes, it does. I just want to make sure that I've captured all of the points you've covered," Alex looked down at his notes.

Trap 2: The Money Trap

Why?

1. We have a money myopia, which causes us to live in the now.
2. We fall into competitive consumption and try to 'keep up with the Joneses.'
3. We are in denial, and believe that worst-case scenarios don't apply to us.

Conventional Approach

Set a budget; be disciplined.
Exercise restraint.

Epiphany Breakthrough

Make eliminating debt fun, interesting, and motivating by turning it into a game. Involve family members in creating a scoreboard to display in your home.

"You know," Alex said, "this conversation has been really beneficial for me. Thank you, Victoria. It's just what I've been missing."

Victoria smiled back. "Happy to be of assistance, my young trapologist. I can't wait to hear what you do with it. And by *you*— I mean Michael and Laura as well," Victoria added.

"I'm right with you, Victoria! I think they'll like this idea," Alex responded.

Victoria noticed that Alex appeared less stressed and burdened. There was a new spark in his eye.

"I know you're headed back to in a few days, but it feels too soon to say goodbye. Would you like to meet up one last time before you go?"

"Of course! I've got a lot to think about with these traps, but I'm glad we've covered everything," Alex replied with a sigh of relief.

"Well, I didn't say that," Victoria said with a wink as she closed the door.

Alex was a bit disconcerted by Victoria's final comment, but overall he left her home in high spirits. He couldn't believe he hadn't recognized the power of these principles before. He knew the effectiveness of a scoreboard to motivate his sales team at work, but he had never connected the dots and applied it at home. He couldn't wait to share what he'd learned with his kids and unveil his plan. He knew Michael would think his dad had lost his marbles and would share what had happened with Kim. But Alex didn't mind. In fact, he hoped Michael would do just that.

* * *

On the way back, Alex finally had the chance to read Chaz's message. *What had been so urgent?* he wondered. It turned out that it was a simple request to RSVP to the company luncheon next month. Oh brother!

When Alex got back to his hotel room, his kids were fighting over the price of their breakfast. Laura had insisted on getting the buffet so she could choose from a lot of options, but Michael felt the price was extravagant at $29.95. Michael's breakfast, which cost him $8.50, consisted of a bagel and orange juice. Alex viewed the disagreement with fresh eyes, seeing himself and his wife in their children. It was really strange to observe them with new eyes.

Laura asked Alex to weigh in on the breakfast. He shocked his daughter when he said, "Honey, $29.95 is really expensive, just for breakfast."

"See, I told you, Laura," Michael said smugly. Alex had never once before agreed with Michael when it came to the cost of a purchase.

"What's happened to you?" Laura asked intently. "Ever since you've been off to see Victoria you've changed."

"Change isn't always a bad thing," Alex responded.

"You're starting to freak me out, Dad," snapped Laura. "I don't know if I like what that lady is doing to you."

Alex cocked his head thoughtfully to one side as he met her gaze. "She's helping me realize things I've never considered before—and it's good. No, actually, it's *great*!"

"So what did you guys talk about today?" Michael asked as Alex sat down on the coach next to him.

"Well, she's helped me label my problems and challenges as *traps*."

"Traps?" the kids asked in unison.

"Traps," Alex confirmed.

"So, what kind of trap has got you, Dad?" Laura asked, suppressing a smile. "A bear trap?"

"You wish," laughed Alex. "So far Victoria has observed two traps—the relationship trap, which I told you about yesterday, and the money trap, which we talked about today. But it sounds like she's not done with me yet," sighed Alex, remembering her parting words.

"Wait—you're not kidding?" said Laura. "I've got to hear this."

"Well, I've been the worst offender when it comes to debt, especially credit card debt," Alex admitted. "I mean, even this trip is being paid for with a new credit card."

"So? What's wrong with that?" Laura pressed.

"In the past, I admit, I saw nothing wrong with it," Alex said evenly. "But I have mountains of debt, and no means to pay for it any time soon. I'm paying a huge amount of interest every single month. It's a lot of pressure."

"So what's going to change now? Are you going to become boring like Michael and never have any fun?" Laura bemoaned.

"No, Laura. The happiest times of my life are spent with you, Michael, and your mom. But right now, I'm spending most of my life paying interest on my debt. If all of that debt was paid off, we could allocate a portion of my income to vacation and travel. That's one of our favorite things to do together," Alex answered.

"So, Dad, how do you get out of debt?" Michael said with interest.

"That's the coolest part, Michael. Victoria suggested we create a scoreboard to track our progress. We represent the $50,000 of credit card debt we've accumulated with a paper snake, which we can hang up in our house and start cutting away as we pay off the debt."

"You have $50,000 in credit card debt?" Michael asked in disbelief. "How is that even possible?"

"Oh, it's possible," Alex responded. "It will be $55,000 by the end of this trip."

"Wow. That's a *lot* of money," Michael pondered aloud.

"Yes, it is," Alex acknowledged. "But it's not all bad! I think that if we scoreboard that debt we can eliminate it in 12 to 18 months."

Laura rolled her eyes. "Yeah, like that's going to happen!" she snapped.

Alex ignored his daughter's negative comment. "Listen," he said, looking at Michael, "if we put $3,000 a month toward our credit card debt and don't add any additional debt, we can do it."

Louder, and with more sass, Laura blurted, "And all of this is going to magically happen because of a paper snake? And we'll all live happily ever after!"

"Hey, I was a little skeptical as well," Alex said to Laura, "but—"

"I love the idea, Dad," Michael interrupted. "I can't wait to create our debt snake."

Alex grinned. "I was hoping you would say that, Michael. I think it would be best to make the snake nice and long. What do you think? Once we've cut out the shape of the snake, we'll mark it at 55 one-inch increments, $1,000 each, to designate the $55,000."

"I want to start making it now!" Michael exclaimed as he leapt from the bed. He grabbed Laura by the elbow. "Laura, come with me, okay?" She moaned as Michael pulled her toward the door. "We'll be right back, Dad," Michael said enthusiastically.

20 minutes later they returned with butcher paper from the hotel kitchen, as well as three 12-inch rulers and some markers from the front desk. Michael did the math to figure out the dimensions.

"How about we make each $1,000 chunk two inches long so we can really see it shrinking?" Michael inquired.

"The faster the better," responded Laura with a grim shake of her head.

"Let's see, that would make it 110 inches long, not counting the head," he said, scribbling the numbers on a scrap of the butcher paper.

"If we make the head 10 inches long, then we are talking a 10-foot snake!" Laura interjected.

Michael nodded in agreement as he marked the dimensions on the long strip of paper. Laura then took over, giving the snake shape and form. Together they worked on the head, making its jaws gape open, as if it was ready to eat them alive. Michael added sharp fangs and a long tongue. Laura drew beady little eyes, then colored them red and drew a furrow in the brow above them. All in all, it was quite a malicious looking creature!

Alex enjoyed sitting back to observe the two of them take charge of the project. Hardly any time had passed since Alex introduced the concept, and already the snake was complete and ready to post on the wall back home! He shook his head in amazement.

At home previously, Alex and Kim had tried to have family meetings to talk about their financial situation and the need to set up a budget. But it had never worked—largely because he himself wouldn't support it. Now, seeing his kids buy into the debt-elimination plan, he felt inspired. Michael was all for it from the start, and Laura had seemed to warm up to it as she helped create the paper snake.

"Why not hang it up in the hotel room while we're here?" Laura suggested, looking in Alex's direction. He smiled in agreement. She turned to Michael and said, "Let's get tape from the front desk when we take back the rulers and markers." Alex could hardly believe what he had just witnessed.

As Laura and Michael fixed their creation to the wall, Michael asked his father, "Is there any way we don't have to go another $5,000 in debt for this trip?"

"Well, probably not," Alex said. "Your flights were $600 a piece. I came on points. The room is close to $400 a night for five nights—we got two nights free as part of a promotion."

"That makes it $3,200 total so far, Dad," Michael calculated quickly.

"That's right! I figured we would spend another $1,800 or so on food, transportation, and entertainment."

Michael was curious. "So, how much have we spent so far on the extras?"

"Well, we got here on Saturday, and it's now Wednesday," Alex said as he was thumbed through his receipts lying on the table.

"Here, Michael. You're better at this than I am. Why don't you add up these receipts?"

"Sure," said Michael. He reached for his phone to open the calculator. In a couple of minutes, he was back with a figure.

"So far, $543.96," he belted out.

"Wow, that's a lot," remarked Laura.

"We spent $151.12 at Roy's, $175.89 at Tommy Bahamas, $124.50 at that fish place, and the sushi place we ate at last night cost us $92.45," said Michael as he shuffled through the receipts."

"Ouch," said Alex. "And how much extra have we spent at the hotel?"

"I think we can access a record of our hotel charges on the TV," Michael offered. "Let me see if I can find out that amount."

After a few minutes, Michael returned with a total of $325.55. He noticed that seven non-alcoholic piña coladas were charged to their account, costing $75.00. He turned to Laura and asked, "Did you seriously get piña coladas every single day?"

"Sort of," Laura admitted. "One on Saturday, two on Sunday, and two on Tuesday . . . so far as I can remember."

"Three on Sunday!" said Michael. "You have to count the one you drank at Tommy's."

"Well, what am I supposed to do in Hawaii if not order piña coladas at Tommy's?" Laura defended herself.

"So that extravagance brings us to . . . $869.51," Michael announced.

"Not bad! We've got over $900.00 and another three days to spend it," Alex said, slipping back to his old self.

"What if we only spent $430.00 in the next three days so that you would only be $54,500 in debt instead of $55,000?" Michael asked.

"That would allow us to cut $500.00 off of the paper snake—an entire inch," Alex observed.

"Every inch counts," Laura laughed.

"Sure, why not! You both have been awesome. Thank you so much for your support!"

"Well, it's not like it was that hard." Laura seemed to brush his comment off. But then she added, with a smile, "Not spending so much going forward will be the hard part."

"Hey, what do you say we hit the beach while we still have some sunlight?"

Alex and the kids quickly changed and headed to the beach behind the hotel. There was a new sense of camaraderie as they jostled each other in the elevator and splashed around in the surf. The sun was out, the water was warm, and the waves were just right for body surfing. Alex could not recall having a better time hanging out with his kids. With this thought, he felt a pang of sadness and regret. He really missed Kim. The family didn't feel complete when she wasn't there.

As the sun started to set, the horizon came alive with color. Laura pointed it out to her dad and brother as they lay on their towels. Alex reflected on how transformational this day had been. He could hardly wait to see what tomorrow had in store. Once more he found himself wishing Kim were here, taking it all in. He wondered how she was feeling and what she might be going through. Michael's next question brought him back.

"Hey Dad, what are we doing for dinner? I'm starving!"

After several hours of playing and swimming in the ocean, they were all pretty exhausted and most definitely ready to eat. It felt good to change out of their swimsuits and put on some fresh casual clothes.

"Okay, how about we get dinner at the local food trucks tonight? The food is really good, some of it is actually gourmet! Better yet, it's less expensive than most restaurants here. They've got Mexican, Chinese, Thai, and the best Hawaiian shrimp you've ever had. The best part is we can all choose something different and meet back at the picnic tables in the center to eat."

Laura went for Thai, Michael for Mexican, and Alex settled down to a large plate overflowing with sticky rice and garlic butter shrimp. It was delicious! And the conversation was a delight, as they talked about their plans and teased each other about who had made the wisest choice. Just for fun, Michael collected everyone's receipts to tally the amount they'd spent when the meal was done. They were thrilled to find that they had spent a fraction of what one of their fancier meals had cost, and yet they'd enjoyed it more than ever. Perhaps this new approach could work after all.

Trap 3: The Focus Trap

On their last morning in Hawaii, Alex went for another run along the beach as he made his way to Victoria's.

"Alex! So great to see you again! You've gotten a lot of sun while you've been here. Haven't you ever heard of sunscreen?" she joked.

"Yeah, I know. My kids have teased me about it. They say I only have two colors—white and red. So I'm embracing the redness while it lasts."

"Well, let me give you some of my pure aloe vera, straight from the plant. It should take some of that burn from your face."

"Thanks for having me here again, Victoria. You've been so kind to share your time and insights with me. I'm sad our trip didn't overlap with Rob being here; it would have been nice to see him again. But it's been really nice to spend time with you."

"Sure thing, Alex, just don't get too dependent on me," Victoria winked as she handed him another smoothie. This one had a strange color and a disconcerting consistency, Alex noticed with dismay.

"Not again. I'm sorry, Victoria. You're so nice to make me this, but I can't do it anymore. Don't make me drink this!"

"It's amazing you're not dead yet, my friend, with all the garbage you've put in your body. Just drink it, it will do you good."

Alex looked at her, looked down at the smoothie, and looked up beseechingly.

But he found no mercy. "Drink!" Victoria insisted.

Alex grimaced then took a big gulp. He swallowed. To his great surprise, he found that it didn't taste as bad as it looked. He raised his eyebrows. "Not . . . poisonous . . ." he admitted, shrugging his shoulders. Victoria kept her gaze fixed on him until he tipped his head back and finished it off.

"Ungrateful little . . ." Victoria muttered, shaking her head as they went inside the house.

"You may have the palate of a five-year-old, Alex, but I'm still glad we were able to meet one last time before you leave paradise," said Victoria.

"I wish I could extend our stay . . ." Alex trailed off, "but duty calls."

"That may be so, but I want you to gain a completely new and different vision about your work and home life. Hopefully you will, once we get into this next trap."

"All right I'm listening," he said, leaning forward.

"The third trap is the Focus Trap, and its main danger is—*being mired in the thick of thin things*," she said.

"Well now, there's some alliteration for you—*the thick of thin things*," Alex mused.

"I learned that phrase from a wise spiritual leader who loves to use alliteration, as a matter of fact."

"So what does it mean?" Alex pressed.

"Thin things are the nonessentials in life," she continued. "They pull at our attention but don't contribute to our purpose. And being caught in *the thick of thin things* suggests that we—like most people—

become absorbed in the superficial, trivial things of life," Victoria clarified.

"You see, Alex, most people are obsessed with getting everything done, executing their to-do list, being in the activity loop. They're caught on the treadmill of life, being constantly *on*, so much so that they haven't distinguished between what's important and what's not. They haven't considered what matters most, or asked themselves to identify their top priorities." Victoria stopped to gauge Alex's expression.

"When you haven't given serious thought and reflection to what you value most," Victoria warned, "everything—both important and trivial—gets lumped together. In reality, Alex, trivial matters end up getting most of our attention, because truly important pursuits require us to be proactive. The things that matter most often require action, to step outside of our normal routine and create space in our schedule so that we can focus. Otherwise, we become overwhelmed by the minutiae of everyday life and other people's agendas," Victoria continued.

"Alex, you've started making some pretty profound changes in your life. You've had the opportunity to reflect upon what's important to you—the essentials. Can you share with me what you perceive as the most critical things in your life?" Victoria asked.

"Sure, but I might need to think about it," Alex answered.

"Great, that's fine. Why don't you spend five minutes writing down what you consider to be most valuable in your life? Don't judge your list—just record thoughts or impressions that come to you. You can shorten your list or add to it later," Victoria suggested.

After five minutes of reflection and silence, Alex's list started to take shape:

- Kim, Laura, and Michael
- Starting my own business
- Exercise
- Eight hours of sleep

- Vacations
- Relationships with my extended family and friends
- Spirituality
- Reading great books
- Meditation and reflection
- Golfing with Chaz

Victoria interrupted the silence, "All right! Your five minutes are up."

"That went by really fast," Alex sighed.

"Anything on the list that surprised you?" Victoria wondered.

"Yes, the second thing on my list was 'starting my own business.' I didn't realize how important that is to me." Alex said

"Tell me more about that," Victoria plied.

"Well, for as long as I can remember, I've wanted to own my own business, but I haven't ever done anything about it. And now I'm in my forties. If I don't do it soon, then I don't know if I'll ever go for it," Alex shared.

"What's kept you from making the break?" she queried.

"Well maybe, in a strange way, I've been trapped by my success at work. Right when I think I'll make a break for it, I get offered a promotion that's too good to turn down, further entrenching me in my career. I keep looking for the right time to make my move, but it never seems to come. I don't know if there ever will be a 'perfect time' to start my business. I just know that the longer I delay, the harder leaving will become," Alex lamented.

"I can tell you that if you trust your instincts you'll know when it's your time to leave," Victoria encouraged.

"I certainly hope so."

Victoria turned back to Alex's list. "Well tell me this—did you see anything on your list about being constantly on top of the latest sports scores?"

Alex shook his head sheepishly. He remembered how Victoria had looked at him when he had pulled out his phone during the middle of their first conversation. Should have seen that one coming, Alex thought.

"Anything about being the first to respond to an email?"

Alex disagreed with her on that one, "Well hold on there, I've got to keep up at work, Victoria. How am I going to do my job, if I'm not checking my email?"

"Ah, Alex," Victoria replied, "We'll get back to that one in a bit. I want you to consider something. When it comes down to it, there are three reasons why we get mired in the thick of thin things."

We Don't Filter What Comes at Us

"We have so much information coming at us that it's impossible to take everything in. Many people try to process it all, but no matter how hard they try they ultimately end up frustrated. It's simply too much! We are continually and perpetually connected to the Internet and the electronic world—a world that is filled with very thin things—and we enter default mode, allowing our attention to be pulled toward whatever is loudest, or brightest, or has the most immediate payoff. There is no filter to separate things that actually deserve our attention from those that merely distract us.

"We also lack patience. We are the 'fast food' generation, where fast is never fast enough. We expect things to happen in our desired timeframe, with little consideration for their natural course. We fail to realize that the best of things take time and aren't instantaneously accessible.

"During the last 20 years our world has changed dramatically. The Internet, email, and social media have begun to dominate our lives. When I was growing up, Alex, if people wanted to get ahold of you they only had three options—a face-to-face visit, a landline telephone call, or a letter by mail. Today, there are innumerable ways to connect, many instantaneous. In the past, if a business associate wanted to contact you, they would reach out between 9 a.m. and 5 p.m. on a business day. Today's environment is 24/7 and 365 days a year. There is never a time when we can't be reached by email or text, and the expectation and impulse to respond immediately is completely out of control," Victoria explained.

"The traditional boundaries that once existed between our work environment and personal life have totally disappeared. What's worse is that we don't filter what comes at us in this context. Our typical approach to this incoming deluge is not to cut out or reduce the flow, but instead to try to manage it all. And yet the flood of information and the demands on our time become more pressing and overpowering. We end up feeling overwhelmed, and important things start to fall through the cracks. We need a new approach. What we are doing now is not sustainable. We can't continue to live at this frenzied pace— something has to give."

Our Digital World Is Full of Thin Things

"We live in a digital world that is completely obsessed with irrelevant information and activity. And we are just now beginning to assess the damage of being perpetually connected to that virtual world." Victoria spoke with conviction as Alex listened.

"I just read a study which found that people in the United States check their social media accounts 17 times a day.[1] Alex, that's once every waking hour on average—if not more often. Isn't that alarming? Think of all that wasted time and focus."

Alex's mind wandered to the countless times he'd found his kids with their eyes glued to their phone screens, times when they could have been outside enjoying nature, reading a book, or spending time with friends.

Victoria thought about the live sports notifications Alex received by the minute.

"Hey, it's not like I'm updating Facebook every day. I'm good," Alex said proudly.

"Sure, Alex. But social media is not the only thing that can be harmful. Being constantly connected to our devices—whether by social media, Internet use, or otherwise—conditions us to expect immediacy in all things. As I mentioned earlier, we live in a *now* era, where we expect everything to be readily available—the moment we decide we want it. Be it the answer to our question, the food we are craving, or the love we are waiting for—we have been conditioned to *now*."

Alex nodded in agreement. "I can't remember when I last had a question that didn't get satisfied almost immediately—well, at least until I met you! You've made me wait days to hear about each of these traps."

Victoria smiled. "I'm just helping you become more aware of how you have been conditioned. Because we access information through the Internet so quickly we begin to expect the same expectation from the people around us. Why haven't they answered yet? When will we get a response? But simply because we *can* be accessible, doesn't mean we ought to be.

"There are just too many outlets for connectivity and entertainment available—each with their own set of obligations and social rules. These distractions fill our precious time with *thin* things—time wasters—leaving the *thick* things of true substance on the back burner or forgotten entirely. What this means is we willingly trade long-term payoff for immediate gratification. Let that sink in for a second."

Alex rubbed his chin with his hand, pondering it all. "It's crazy that life as a kid today is so different than it used to be, you know?

"Kids used to entertain themselves by playing with friends, reading books, using their imagination, spending time exploring outdoors—at least that's how it was for Bobby and me when we were young," he continued. "Even here in Hawaii—Laura and Michael's attention gets stolen away by their screens. What ever happened to good-old-fashioned playtime?" Alex demanded.

"It's scary, huh? Our reality has changed. I was just reading a report where a doctor said he 'found it easier to treat heroin and crystal meth addicts than lost-in-the-matrix video gamers or Facebook-dependent social media addicts.'[2] Doesn't that make you want to chuck your kids' phones into the ocean? And throw out your own along with them?"

"Completely!" Alex agreed, "But it's just not realistic."

"Why couldn't it be?" Victoria retorted. "Alex, you can create your own reality. This constant connection, this overuse of something so thin as staring at a screen, is harmful and unproductive.

"There's a reason why parents who work as tech professionals often enroll their kids in Montessori or tech-free schools. Scientists don't call screens *electronic cocaine* for no reason. It's a serious problem that has infiltrated our modern world. The effects are pervasive on our attention and productivity."

"Wow, all of this is hard to hear. My kids could totally use a break from their electronics," Alex sighed.

"Alex, your kids aren't the only ones who could use a break. You might try looking a little closer to home. In our short time together, I've noticed how often you check your phone unconsciously. Your fingers even move unwittingly to your most used apps," Victoria said gently. "You might consider a digital scale-back yourself."

Alex was about to protest, but realized he had no defense. He had felt the allure of his phone grow weaker in the past week, but he knew it would be a hard pull to resist upon returning home. He would need to take stock and establish some new habits and control mechanisms. He didn't want to miss a moment of the best that life had in store for him, just because he couldn't resist being sucked in by a screen.

The Best Things in Life Take Time

"Anything that is worthwhile in life takes time and requires our commitment and effort," Victoria continued, as she moved into the third reason for falling into the Focus Trap. "Alex, I want you to spend five minutes making a list that includes the accomplishments you are most proud of."

"Okay, sure."

As Alex faced this challenge, he came up with three things he felt represented his greatest accomplishments, at least up to this point in his life. He opened the red journal and jotted them down:

Family—Kim, Laura, and Michael
Professional work achievements
Relationship with God

"Now, Alex, when you look at the three things you wrote, do you find any common characteristics that make them more important compared to other things that didn't make the list?" Victoria asked.

"Well, that's an interesting question. I see the common thread to be relationships—whether with God, my family, or my work associates. They seem to be more important than anything else," Alex responded.

"Nice summary," Victoria smiled. "And in your view, what's the key ingredient for a successful relationship?"

After thinking for a moment, Alex responded, "I would say it's a healthy balance of give and take, working together as a team, and spending quantity as well as quality time together."

"You spend a week in Hawaii and suddenly you are a genius," Victoria teased. "I believe you're right. All three of those factors are critical, and validate my point about prioritizing relationships. The more time we invest in our relationships, the more we will appreciate them.

Conventional Approach

"The conventional approach to the Focus Trap doesn't attempt to address our existing reality—the reality where we live in information overload, overscheduled and overcommitted to far too many thin things. This approach doesn't question or filter the information coming at us.

"Instead, the conventional approach tries to manage it all. This approach says 'yes' to everything and 'no' to nothing. This approach says you can do and have it all. There are no tradeoffs that need to be made. There are no limits on the number of balls that we have in the air. Instead, we just have to improve our juggling skills."

"Of course," Victoria continued, "the current approach is not working. By trying to be all things to all people we end up compromising our health and relationships. We become completely unfocused. We aren't able to deliver on the most important things in our life. We end up being the caretaker of minutiae rather than the purpose-driven architect of our life.

"We experiment with system after system that promise to be the answer to help us get control and manage all the information and complexity coming at us. Because the current environment has become unmanageable our system becomes an ad-hoc system that promises everything but fails to deliver on the things we care most about."

Epiphany Breakthrough

"The epiphany breakthrough is fundamentally different from the current, conventional approach," Victoria said. "Instead of trying to manage everything coming at us, we must first filter out the unimportant and trivial, so that we can then spend our time on our most critical goals. We must be proactive about our decisions, say no to the persistent and sticky minutiae, and accept that we can't do it all.

"We must learn to detach from the thin things in our lives. This requires a lot of discipline because these things often provide short-term diversion or lend a false sense of accomplishment. We need to examine our habits carefully, making sure we aren't repeatedly caught up in these diversions . . . We can't just ignore them—we have to identify and detach from them. Otherwise the unimportant will stick to us and become an automatic part of our routines."

"Can you give me an example?" Alex asked.

"Yes. Recently, I found that my email box was full of advertisements and deals from various companies. And I'm not talking about spam. I have an email filter that blocks out all my spam. These emails were from restaurants I frequented, stores I bought products from, airlines I flew on, and hotels I stayed at.

"Now it didn't seem like a big deal, but I was receiving 15 to 20 emails a day from these various companies. I decided I needed to detach myself from these advertisements, so I went to each and every email that generated the emails and unsubscribed. It was totally liberating, Alex. A week transpired and I opened up my inbox to find no emails like that waiting for my attention. It felt liberating to eliminate the clutter, like I was spring cleaning my house or gutting my garage," explained Victoria.

"Makes sense. I'm going to do that once I get back home," Alex responded.

"You plan to, but I guarantee there will be a thousand things to pull you off target. I think you'll find that—as important as it is to create your daily or weekly to-do-list—it is equally important to create your not-to-do-list," said Victoria.

"Your not-to-do-list?" Alex was puzzled.

"Yes, your list of things to not do—call it your nonessentials list. Identify what's keeping you from getting to what's most important, what's distracting and interrupting you throughout the day.

"Alex, our whole life is about staying on target, moving toward those things that matter most while not allowing ourselves to be derailed or thrown off course. We need to nip distractions in the bud from the very beginning, before they can get root. Each week we need to start with a clean slate and then strategically add what is most important to our calendar, while confidently ignoring and detaching ourselves from the trivial and unimportant things that try to distract us. Of course, this is easier said than done."

Alex sighed in agreement.

"Learning to say no goes against the cultural norms and expectations of our society. There is an unwritten social expectation to never say no. In fact, we are initially rewarded for saying yes. But, by doing so, we inevitably suffer the consequences of being overcommitted and overwhelmed. And thus in the end, we disappoint those who had just been praising us for saying yes.

"When we view our life and work from the context that 10 percent is important and 90 percent is unimportant, we can begin to realize how mired in minutiae we may have become. Most of the things that occupy our minds and consume our days are truly unimportant. But by recognizing this, we can move to the liberating concept that we have a choice. We don't have to accept life as it is handed to us. I like how Steve Jobs put it—'It's only by saying no that you can concentrate on the things that are really important.'"[3]

Alex checked his journal to make sure he had captured all the main points.

Trap 3: The Focus Trap

Why?

1. We have too much coming at us—we don't filter what merits our energy, time, and attention.
2. We are perpetually connected to the Internet and the electronic world—most of this world consists of very thin things.
3. We lack patience and expect things to happen on our timeframe—immediately, if not sooner. We fail to recognize, or we forget, that the best things in life take time and are not instantaneous.

Conventional Approach

An approach that suggests we can manage everything coming at us by learning to become a better juggler. This approach doesn't attempt to reduce the number of balls we have in the air. Rather, it suggests that we should develop the skills to juggle all the balls we have in the air (a metaphor for everything in our life).

Epiphany Breakthrough

The epiphany breakthrough occurs when we realize that we can't do it all. We have to filter out the unimportant, detach from the minutiae, and learn to say "no" more often so that we can say "yes" to the things we value most.

Alex felt like the concepts were beginning to gel in his mind, although he knew it would be a process that would take time and practice to master.

Victoria's voice cut in on his musings. "Alex, I'm impressed with your willingness to make lasting changes in your life for the better. It's not like I have all the answers, I'm just a little further down the path than you are. I speak from experience in the hope that you can avoid the pitfalls I myself have fallen into." Victoria paused, gauging her next words.

"I realize that much of what I've shared with you is new and different. I'm not asking you to take my word for it. Test it out. Try it. Experiment for yourself. And see if your experience resonates with what I've been saying."

Alex nodded appreciatively.

"I hope you have an uneventful trip home tonight on the red-eye. Let's keep in touch. I want to hear all about your progress as you extricate yourself from the three traps we've discussed. Remember: if you ever need encouragement, don't hesitate to give me a call. If I don't pick up immediately, you'll know I am at yoga, the beach, or whipping up one of those delicious smoothies you have come to love so much."

Alex raised an eyebrow, but resisted the snide remark that came to mind.

"I will get back to you eventually, never fear," Victoria smiled. "In fact, I have a conference coming up in Los Angeles this summer. Maybe we could get together to assess your progress when I am stateside?"

"I would love to stay connected, Victoria. Our time together has been revelatory, and this vacation has been much different than I anticipated. I have a lot to think over and some big decisions to make," Alex shared.

"Be patient with the process, Alex, and realize that it will take time for these changes to stick. But I'll be here to support and help you in any way I can," Victoria reassured him.

"Thank you. And give my best to Rob—I hope I get to see him next time we meet up," Alex said.

"Will do. Please give my best to Laura, Michael, and Kim, when you see her next," Victoria said.

"Goodbye, Victoria."

"All the best, Alex! You will be a certified trapologist before you know it!" Victoria smiled and waved after him as he headed back down the beach.

Alex arrived back to an empty hotel room around noon. He had requested a late checkout, as their flight didn't leave until 10 p.m. that night, but he expected his kids to be lounging in the hotel room when he got back. He figured they must be at their favorite spot, further down the beach close to a rock jetty. Michael would spend hours trying to catch the small, incredibly speedy crabs that found shelter in the nooks and crannies of the lava rock. They had even been lucky enough to spot a sea turtle hiding there in the reef. Alex walked down to the beach, and sure enough, there they were.

"Hi guys! How is the surf?" Alex shouted out.

"Best waves of the whole week!" Michael responded.

"Dad, watch me ride this one in," Laura shouted. She caught the next wave with impeccable timing and coasted smoothly into shore.

"Wow! You rode that baby all the way! Nice going, Laura."

"So, how was your time with Victoria?" Laura asked as she pulled herself up from the sand.

"Awesome, as usual," Alex smiled.

"Did you she tell you about the third trap?" Laura asked.

"Yes, as a matter of fact, she did. It's about being mired in the thick of thin things," Alex said.

"Well, are you mired in the thick of . . . whatever you said?" Laura asked.

"You know better than to ask that question," Alex said, as they walked a little deeper into the ocean.

"So, I'll take that as a yes."

"Affirmative," said Alex.

"Well, are you going to be doing anything about it?" Laura asked.

"Lots of things," Alex said, turning around to face the shore. "Let's talk more about it over dinner. For now, I want to show you two that your old man still knows how to body surf," said Alex. Suddenly, a wave came up from behind, knocked him over, and smashed him onto the sand. He rose up out of the water, sputtering.

"Are you okay, Pops? Don't go all heroic on us. We will take your word for it. We need you to stick around to take care of us," Michael laughed.

"I'll be okay, eventually," Alex said, disoriented as he collapsed on the sand. "I guess the ocean doesn't exactly go easy on a guy."

Michael and Laura smiled and went back out to catch the next wave. Alex decided he didn't have anything to prove, and ducked under the oncoming waves until he felt ready to head back in. It felt great to relax on the warm sand and listen to the sound of the crashing surf. It took him back to when they had first arrived, and the sound of the ocean had soothed his frazzled spirit. In a way, it felt like a lifetime ago; each day here had been so full of insight and enlightenment. He wondered if it would all feel like a dream once he was back in the rat race of life in L.A. How would he navigate this new trajectory that was opening before him?

Later that night at the shrimp food truck, Michael kicked off the conversation: "Okay, fam, do you realize we've spent less than $400 on food and other expenses since Wednesday? We will have achieved our goal of only adding $4,500 additional credit card debt instead of $5,000 to Papa Bear's back." Michael beamed with delight.

"I never thought I would say this, but nice going, Michael," Laura chimed.

"This has been a team effort and I'm expecting your help in cutting that $500 inch off our debt snake when we get back home," Michael said.

"Done deal!" said Laura.

Alex's phone buzzed with a new email notification. He pulled out his phone instinctively, but instead of looking at it, he went into his settings and turned off all notifications. This was his last night with his kids in paradise. The rest could wait.

PART
3 | Traps 4–6

Back to Reality

Once they arrived home, Michael and Laura unzipped their suitcases and carefully unfolded the paper debt snake they had made. Together, each holding one end of its body, they marched to the kitchen, where they proudly displayed the debt snake on the wall for all to see.

Alex was determined to follow through on the commitments he had made in Hawaii, where he had learned so much and felt so liberated. But now that he was back and in the swing of things, he knew it was going to be harder than he'd anticipated, especially when it came to money. Nevertheless, he was laser-focused on eliminating their family debt. Michael was leading the charge, but he still couldn't get over how supportive his daughter was being as well—that, he could not have predicted. He had to stay strong in the game, even if it was just for their sakes.

A few days later, Alex sat in his office at home, lost in thought. Deeply dreading the months ahead, and the effort it would take to fight his way out of the hole he had spent his way into, he propped his elbows on the desk and rested his head in his hands.

Michael knocked softly and poked his head through the door. "Hey Dad," he said, watching as Alex looked up, "are you okay?"

Alex flashed a smile. "Of course! What's up? Come on in."

Michael returned the smile and sat down at the chair in front of Alex's desk. "Well, from one business guy to another, I have a proposition for you."

"I'm listening." Alex was curious.

"Well, I'm guessing that you're probably paying somewhere between 20 to 30 percent interest on those credit cards, huh?"

Alex's smile faded. "Yeah. What about it?" His tone turned sharp. When Michael recoiled, he softened his response. "Sorry, it's just a painful reminder. So, what's your proposition?"

"This morning as I was eating breakfast, I couldn't stop staring at the snake," he confessed. "Mom has always helped me save the money I've earned, from lawn mowing . . . my eBay account . . . money I received for my birthdays . . ." Michael rambled on.

"Okay . . .?" Alex questioned.

"Anyway," said Michael. "I thought I could help you kill the snake." Alex clasped his hands together and leaned in, his eyes focused on Michael.

Michael looked down as he spoke, "I have $18,000 saved up, and I'm only earning a measly $2 or $3 a month in interest right now. So what if I loaned you that money?"

Alex was stunned. Was he dreaming? His 14-year-old kid was offering him money to get out of debt. This had to be a joke Kim had set up. "Michael, are you serious?" he asked. Michael nodded enthusiastically. "That's so generous of you. It would allow me to pay off a third of our credit card debt."

He thought for a second. "But I would only agree to it if you let me pay you some interest. Are you okay with that?"

"Sure," Michael replied coolly, as he tried to mask a big grin spreading across his face.

"I can't believe I'm talking to you of all people about this . . . but I'm happy to take you up on your offer!" Alex grinned at Michael, who exhaled and smiled back at his dad.

"I'll write up an agreement, okay?" Michael said before he rushed out of the room.

Alex laughed out loud to himself—unable to believe this unprecedented turn of events. Thirty minutes later, Michael returned with a document with the interest rate left blank. Alex read over the terms and wrote in an interest rate he thought was fair. Instead of the 20-plus percent interest he was being charged on his credit cards, he would be paying just eight percent annually. Michael had given him 18 months to pay the loan back. In the meantime, he was thrilled to be making some interest income.

Alex fished a black pen out of the desk drawer. He passed it to Michael, who scribbled a confident signature and then slid the pen back to his father. Alex felt a swell of pride—what a smart and solid boy he had. With Michael's $18,000, he would be able to eliminate two of his five credit cards—one of which carried a $10,000 balance and the other an $8,000 balance.

At the bank the next day Alex helped Michael make the transfer. As soon as the money was in his account, he called the two credit card companies to pay off the balances. Now it was time for the ceremonial cutting up of the cards. Michael and Laura insisted on being the ones to do it. The three of them gathered the little pieces and threw them defiantly in the kitchen garbage. This was about taking control back.

Alex felt that everything was taking a positive turn. He felt surprisingly light and free. Then the unthinkable came to his mind—*What if I turned in my new car*? With depreciation, he probably wouldn't get his down payment back, but he would eliminate his monthly car payment, the balance of which could be directly applied to his debt.

He recoiled from the thought and shook his head. Ridiculous. He could never give up his car. *I drive nice cars*, he thought to himself, *that's the kind of man I am*. Besides, what would Chaz think? Alex needed the car to appear successful and prosperous. Without it, how would he be seen by his colleagues at work? He would have to park every day in a different section of the parking lot—away from Chaz's view. It was too much. He deserved to be driving that car. He had paid his dues and this was his reward. No need for guilt, there were other ways to cut back.

With Kim now settled into her new job in San Francisco, she had planned to come home every weekend, or at the very least twice a month. She would stay with her parents when she came into town.

The established arrangement was that Kim would text Alex when she arrived on Friday night, at which point he'd drop off the kids until Sunday evening. Laura and Michael missed their mom. They looked forward to the time they'd get to spend with her over the weekends.

At Kim's first visit, Alex pulled up to his in-laws' home driving his shiny black convertible, fresh from the car wash. Kim didn't even raise her eyes to watch the car approach. Alex waved to her as Laura and Michael slid out of the car, but she didn't wave back. She couldn't stand the sight of Alex sitting proudly at the wheel. Everything to do with that car disgusted her.

The kids ran up to her, and she embraced them. "Laura, Michael! Tell me everything! I want to hear all about Hawaii!" They turned away from the street and walked arm-in-arm into the house.

* * *

Although things were still not positive with Kim, Alex felt surprisingly great to be back at work. He had wondered if his old environment would cause him to fall back into his old patterns. But he was committed to escaping his traps, even if the undertaking was daunting, so he pushed the doubt from his mind.

Alex had started bringing lunch into work each day. He'd been able to eliminate some time-wasting habits and was feeling confident about his spending cuts, but it was really difficult having his office next to Chaz's. Chaz had a habit of turning so-called quick questions into two-hour help-me-fix-this-problem sessions. He was just getting started on a client proposal when Chaz's curly-haired head popped into view.

"What's up, my man? How's that new car working out?"

"Loving it," Alex grinned. "Being faster than your car is just one of the many perks."

"Ahhhh, that's not been proven yet. Hey, I wanted to ask you—do you want to go out for lunch? I heard great things about this hot new sushi restaurant. It's only a 10-minute drive from here," Chaz said, flashing a smile.

"Ah, well, I'm definitely tempted, but I packed a lunch today. I'm trying to cut back on spending a bit," Alex responded.

"Throw me the bag, let's see what garbage the missus put in there." Chaz laughed as he sauntered over to his desk. Alex reluctantly tossed it to him and Chaz began rummaging through its contents.

"This looks like a dog's lunch to me. Come on, let's go grab some real food. Your wife won't care that you didn't eat the lousy lunch she packed."

"I packed it myself. Kim and I have been separated for a few weeks now," Alex said dejectedly.

"You're kidding! Well, no worries, mate. There are a lot of fish in the sea."

Alex raised his eyebrows at Chaz's insensitivity. "We've been married for 20 years, Chaz. That's not something you just throw away."

"Yeah, yeah. It's awesome. Good for you two." It was as if Chaz hadn't even heard what he'd said. "So what do you say? Let's go."

Alex glanced at the brown paper lunch bag. It did look rather pathetic. "Fine, but I've got to be back before 2 p.m.," he cautioned.

"No worries. We'll have you back in a flash," Chaz said confidently. "So, are you going to let me drive your car? I know the way to the sushi place," Chaz asked.

"You break it, you buy it."

"Yeah, whatever—I'll be careful. I haven't had an accident in six months," he winked.

At the sushi restaurant, Chaz ordered three of the most expensive rolls, which totaled nearly $60.00. Meanwhile, Alex enjoyed a California roll and miso soup. Now that his spending habits had changed, he was starting to notice Chaz's glaring extravagance. At least Chaz would be paying this time—he had told the waiter to bring just one check.

When the bill came Chaz snatched it. "I've got this my man." He started to dig through his pockets and even stood up to make a big show of rummaging through his coat. He came up empty-handed.

"Shoot! Looks like I forgot my wallet. I can't believe I did that again. Do you think you can get this today?"

Alex nodded and pulled out his card. He had seen this routine before.

"Thanks, bro! I'll cover us on the next one."

Alex rolled his eyes and sighed as Chaz looked down at his phone. Chaz always talked about "picking up the next one"—which conveniently never seemed to come. Including the tip, lunch came to $82.45. Alex fumed, but said nothing.

As Alex drove back to the office, Chaz checked out his new golf clubs on his cell phone. "Hey, take a look at these—they will add 40 yards to my drive," he bragged, shoving his phone in Alex's face.

"Looks like I'll never be able to keep up with you, Chaz." Alex parked and slid out of the car. "I've got to dash to my meeting."

"2:05! Told you we'd get back on time."

Alex winced as he rushed inside, annoyed that he had allowed Chaz to make him late.

Despite his best intentions, it was really hard for Alex to say no to people who made requests of him. It wasn't unusual for Chaz or his boss to hijack his whole morning or the better part of the day on what they deemed was a crisis. But when Alex had a genuine emergency, neither Chaz nor his boss really reciprocated. This realization annoyed Alex, but to date he hadn't the courage to take a stand.

In Hawaii with Victoria, Alex had felt like he could do anything— get out of debt, repair his relationship with Kim, and regain control of his work life. But it was hard to come home and put it all into action. Sometimes he fell back into his old ways, like the day he stopped by a sports outlet store on the way home from work and spent nearly $600 on running shoes, athletic clothes, and a running jacket. When he opened the trunk to get the bags, however, he felt a pang of guilt for not sticking to his plan. Two days later, he decided to take everything back but couldn't find the receipt. He called the store to see if they would make an exception, but their return policy was strict. No return without a receipt.

Alex tried to rationalize his behavior when he lapsed into his old ways. *How much could I realistically change at once?* He had a hard time turning down golf with Chaz. He still liked to eat out at nice restaurants and still had a preference to hire out the yard work. The momentum he'd had in Hawaii had not only stalled but it seemed to be rapidly moving in reverse.

Back at the house, Alex scrutinized his credit card statements. This was a new habit since he had been back. As a whole, the family's spending had decreased, but there were still some purchases that made him want to scream. Most of them had come from Laura: a purchase on Amazon for $290.63, for starters, and $480.39 at some department store. Had she forgotten everything they'd agreed to?

His mind wandered off to a memory of Laura as a little girl:

"Daddy, Daddy, Daddy," Laura pulled on Alex's hand.

"Yes, princess?" Alex said as he kissed his daughter's blonde head.

"Look at this!" Laura spread a doll magazine on the table in front of Alex and pointed. "I want this one."

"Okay, let's order it after dinner," he said.

"Alex," Kim interjected sharply, "we've already talked about this. We agreed—no more dolls."

"Kim, it's fine . . ." Alex began to respond.

"Laura already has 14 dolls. She's certainly not deprived, and we really can't afford to get any more," Kim said, exasperated.

"But I want this one," Laura said. "Mommy, she looks just like me!"

Kim didn't respond, she just glared at Alex. But still he said, "Okay, princess. Let's talk about it after dinner."

"I want this hat, this outfit, and this bag too," Laura pointed, "that way we can match. She will look just like me!" Laura beamed at the thought.

Alex kissed her cheek, "Okay, now go help your mom set the table."

"Dad. Dad. *Dad*!" Laura's voice brought Alex back to the present. "What's wrong with you? I've said your name like seven times, but you're just sitting there in a daze."

"Oh, sorry. What's up?"

"I need the keys to your car and some money. I'm going out with friends."

"What friends?"

"I'm in a rush right now so I'll tell you later. Where's your wallet?" Laura snapped her fingers waiting for her father to respond.

Alex scowled. "Hey, don't snap your fingers at me. It's over on the kitchen counter."

"Good," said Laura, as she withdrew $100 along with one of his credit cards.

"I hope this one works," Laura muttered to herself as she put the card in her purse. "Thanks, Dad! Don't worry about me for dinner, and don't wait up," she exclaimed as she bounded out the door toward the garage.

"Hey wait," Alex said as he opened the door to the garage. "No later than midnight."

"We'll see," said Laura as she slammed the door.

"Hey, drive safe and be careful with my car!" Alex shouted, but Laura was already gone.

He stood there for a moment, feeling frustrated and discouraged. Laura had seemed so interested in and supportive of the debt snake—why couldn't Alex get through to her now? Her interest had gone cold as soon it began to impact her life. Once Alex clamped down on expenditures, Laura had begun to rebel. She wasn't going to change her life because her dad had suddenly decided to instigate some new program. She was still staying up way too late, missing school, and spending freely. What concerned Alex most is that while she talked a big game about going to college in New York, Laura had yet to pick up a book to study for the SAT or any one of her advanced courses. All she seemed to care about or have time for was going out with her friends.

How do you inspire someone to change? Alex shook his head at the irony of it all. His wife had been trying to get Alex to change for most of their married life with little or no success. Now Alex was attempting the same thing with his daughter, to no avail. He thought Victoria might have a thing or two to say about that. He decided to give her a call.

Trap 4: The Change Trap

"Well, well, well . . . If it isn't my young trapologist. How's the rat race in L.A.?" Alex couldn't help but smile at the sound of Victoria's cheeky voice.

"Oh you know, same ol', same ol'. How are things with you? Still sporting the green mustache?"

"You know it!" Victoria retorted.

Alex gave Victoria a quick update on everything he'd been doing since they last talked, or at least the things he'd been doing well. Most of all he wanted to get Victoria's opinion on the situation with Laura.

"How do you change someone who doesn't want to change?" he asked.

"You don't, Alex. It's that simple."

"Gee thanks, Victoria. That's not exactly helpful."

"Well, I guess there's more to it than that. Look, I'm coming to that conference in L.A. in a couple weeks. Would you like to meet me at my hotel for dinner? We can order room service and chat on my balcony. It's not as nice as Hawaii, but then again, what is? And it will be my treat. How does that sound?"

"Sounds great!" Alex replied enthusiastically.

"Well then, I look forward to seeing you soon. I'll text you when I land and we can pick an evening that's convenient for you. I'll be in town for three days."

The next couple of weeks went by in a flash, and before Alex knew it he was in Victoria's hotel room. It felt good to be back in her company, and Alex was excited to hear what she had to say.

"So Alex, you want to know how you can get Laura to change her ways. But you need to understand something first: You'll find in life that there are two forces at play that move a person to change: the force of conscience or the force of circumstance. Either we act on what we know we need to change, or we are compelled to act by the reality of our circumstances. Unfortunately, most people would rather not alter their behavior, so they ignore their conscience and delay change until the force of circumstance humbles them to deal with whatever crisis is at hand."

Alex remembered how low he had felt that first day in Hawaii, looking over his 34th-story balcony. "That sounds like me, I pretty much hit rock bottom, and I realized I had to do something drastic. Desperate times . . ." he said ruefully.

Victoria looked at him intently. "You were ready to change because of your circumstances, but now you're asking Laura to change because of her conscience. Not impossible, but much more difficult to take action on. She needs to find her own equally powerful motivation to do what she knows in her heart is right. You're trying to be the Jiminy Cricket on her shoulder, and that just won't work."

Alex nodded, musing, "Maybe I should let you talk with her."

"I think you'll find that she's not the only person facing this challenge," she said, winking at Alex. His heart sank. What was that supposed to mean?

Before he could ponder her remark any further, she jumped in. "We both know that food is more essential than talk, so here's a dinner menu. You can't think straight on an empty stomach. Let me know what you'd like to order. Unfortunately my delicious smoothies are not on the menu!"

Alex laughed, secretly relieved, and glanced over the menu. "I'll have the rack of ribs with fries, and a soda," Alex offered.

"I see you're still trying to kill yourself with food," Victoria said, shaking her head. She picked up the phone and dialed room service.

"Hi, dinner for two, please. One rack of ribs, one spinach salad, one soda, and let's see . . . Is your juice fresh squeezed? Hmm. Okay, let's just do water then. Yes, that's it. Thank you!"

Victoria turned back to Alex, "Okay, we've got 30 minutes until the food arrives," she said, gesturing toward the balcony door. They headed outside to a stunning view of the city's twinkling lights. The San Gabriel Mountains framed the scene to the north, and far out to the southwest they caught a glimpse of the Pacific Ocean. They settled into comfortable chairs and enjoyed a quiet moment as the balmy evening breeze washed over them.

"So, let's jump right in," Victoria suggested. "The fourth trap is called the Change Trap. And when we talk about change, we need to talk about what keeps us from making it: procrastination—*the killer of growth and transformation.*"

"Well, this is probably the first trap that hasn't surprised me," Alex responded.

"As I've said, these traps are made especially dangerous by the forces of our modern times, and procrastination is one of the most common, especially when it comes to change. We all have a tendency to put off things that we aren't comfortable doing. We have an even harder time changing our behaviors long-term. We come up with all kind of reasons and excuses to avoid change. Do you remember that study I referred you to earlier?"

"You mean the one where people would rather die than change?" Alex asked.

"Yes, that's the one," Victoria said. "Can you imagine someone literally choosing to die before changing a bad habit?"

"That sounds extreme, but I know a few people who make me believe it!" Alex replied.

"When we put off or avoid the changes we need to make in our life, our growth stagnates and our progress stalls. We become stuck. This is why I call procrastination the *killer* of growth and transformation." Victoria reached for a worn binder with the word TRAPS scribbled on the front in big, block letters. She opened it and thumbed to the tab that read *Change Trap*. "Here's a list I made, with three core reasons why people fall into this trap." Victoria moved the binder so Alex could read.

1. Change is difficult. It can be painful and uncomfortable to change in meaningful ways. It's easier to stay with the familiar and comfortable.
2. Rationalization and postponement. People delude themselves that change can be postponed to a more convenient or appealing time, once they've finished a certain phase of life.
3. Perfectionism. Those who suffer from this malady often live by the mantra, *if I can't be perfect at it then I might as well not even try.*

Change Is Difficult

"Alex, I've explored the research behind why people resist change." She flipped open a new tab in the *Traps* binder.

"Why we resist change: The psychologist Jim Taylor describes the attempt to change as 'swimming against the tide of many years of baggage, habits, emotions and environment.' Taylor observed four major obstacles that inhibit lasting change. I'll summarize this list, Alex, instead of reading the details. First: baggage from the past such as low self-esteem, perfectionism, fear of failure, and anger. Second: deeply ingrained habits in the way we think, experience emotions, and behave. Third: the fear of acting on changes we need to make because we fear failure. Fourth: the environment and activities we participate in, which give us a sense of the comfort and security from which it is difficult to break free.[1]

"As Taylor summarizes—and here I will quote him again: 'Fighting change is a self-preservation instinct. If we successfully avoid change, we successfully manage our baggage and protect what we know, or our way of life. If we don't have to face the unflattering failures, we don't have to experience painful, frustrating self-examination required for our betterment.'"[2]

Victoria finished reading from her trap binder and glanced at Alex to assess his reaction. He was nodding his head thoughtfully.

"I guess I've been all too successful at self-preservation in the past—I am a master procrastinator!" Alex laughed ruefully. "It hurts, but it fits. And I guess the truth, albeit painful, can be liberating in the right time and place."

"Alex, people will do everything in their power to avoid change. It's human nature. As you've probably heard, it takes 21 days to change a habit.[3] Good habits require us to be proactive and take initiative, whereas bad habits usually don't require much resourcefulness from us. That's why it takes so long to change bad habits," she explained.

"Makes sense," agreed Alex.

Rationalization and Postponement

"Alex, if you don't have any questions on the first reason why change is difficult, let's move on to the second point: Even when people know they need to change, they look for all kinds of rationalizations to delay those changes until eventually their circumstances force them to do so.

Okay—so we're back to the concept of being humbled by either force of circumstance or force of conscience." she continued.

"Yeah, we were talking about Laura, right?"

"Right! Most people will not change until circumstances compel them to. Think of your resistance to curbing your debt. For your entire marriage, Kim has tried to get you to avoid debt. But how did you respond?" Victoria asked.

"I ignored her because I wasn't convinced it was necessary to change. I thought my way of doing things was superior to hers," Alex said.

"Often, we value the opinions of those closest to us the least," Victoria's said softly.

"Why do you think that is?" he asked.

"Because we get stuck in a rut, become a slave to our habits, and overlook the feelings and concerns of our loved ones. We essentially take their opinion for granted. What caused you to eventually change after more than 20 years of cajoling?" Victoria asked.

"Two things. First, my income was dramatically reduced, and second, Kim left to pursue that job in San Francisco. That was a real shock," Alex confessed.

"That's a prime example of being humbled by your circumstances. Your lowered pay and separation from Kim forced you to address this problem—this *trap*."

"You're right," Alex admitted. "But what do I do? How do I avoid more of the pain and agony I've been through? How do I make the change necessary before I'm compelled to be humble?"

"You avoid it by listening to your conscience and course-correcting before things get out of hand. Alex, your conscience teaches you right from wrong. It is that little voice inside of you that tries to steer you clear of danger or disaster. We tend to let the sheer noise and busyness of life drown out the voice of conscience. And because it is a small voice, we're not able to hear it unless we're paying attention. We all need to take proactive measures to understand that inner voice, to let it teach and guide us. Some of these measures include pausing to pray, reflect, meditate, and listen."

"It's interesting that something so simple can have such a powerful effect," Alex mused.

"When we are in tune with our conscience, we are able to make the necessary course corrections in our lives before our circumstances require us to. This is what I mean by the *force of conscience*," Victoria explained. "And the more we listen and respond to that conscience, the more educated and effective we will be!

"You know, Alex, I rely daily on my conscience to help me navigate life. And it has never steered me wrong. The only time I get off course is when I ignore that inner voice. Whether I've neglected to take the proactive measures we talked about, or have chosen simply to ignore what my conscience is telling me because I don't want to hear it in that moment—either way I've ended up suffering the consequences for a bad decision that could have been avoided."

"I find it hard to believe that you've made very many bad decisions," Alex interjected.

"Actually, the poor decisions I've made throughout my life are the reason I can now share these insights with you. At some point, I've fallen prey to each and every one of these traps. They feel so vivid and poignant because I've personally experienced the pain and anguish they produce," she revealed.

Victoria was interrupted by the sound of the doorbell—their dinner had arrived.

Perfectionism

Between her bites of salad and his mouthfuls of pork, Victoria and Alex continued their conversation.

Actually, Victoria was keen to do most of the talking. "Perfectionism, the third reason people procrastinate and avoid change, is an inhibiting philosophy that millions of people cling to," she told Alex. "It's damaging mainly because it directly conflicts with the way we learn—by trying and experimenting, or falling and getting back up again, just like a toddler learning to walk. This is how we grow and develop in life. But perfectionism gives no allowance for mistakes or for trial and error.

"I've suffered for much of my life from habitual perfectionism," she admitted, glancing downward. "It was deeply rooted in my psyche and very much a part of my upbringing. My father was the same way—he was very hard on himself, and making mistakes or falling short was unacceptable. I avoided starting new things, like learning to play the piano or studying a new language, because of this. It has been said that practice is the best of all instructors. Perfectionists often don't allow themselves to practice at something, but expect to be perfect right out of the gate.

"Consider perfectionism objectively. What if we had quit trying to walk as a toddler, or spoke only words we could pronounce perfectly? That might sound silly, but here's what I mean: Perfectionism is an acquired trait, not inherent in human development, at least until we become susceptible to it at a certain age. If we were born perfectionists, we would never play any sport, never learn an instrument, and certainly never learn a second language. We would take jobs and positions only when success was guaranteed.

"You see, it's unrealistic to expect we'll accomplish anything significant without many failures prior to experiencing success. But we witness this kind of self-punishing behavior all the time in people who refuse to change a behavior or habit because it will make them look bad. As a perfectionist there is nothing worse than looking bad in front of others," Victoria said.

"Yeah, you've described a situation I see frequently. It's not a particular challenge for me, but I think Michael struggles with this."

"Is that so? Tell me how perfectionism manifests itself in Michael's life."

"Well, as you know, Michael is a lot more like Kim than me," Alex said.

"And we can thank God for that," Victoria smiled. He chose to ignore her teasing and continued on.

"Michael is very careful and conservative. He doesn't like taking risks. And when he tries something new or different, he exhaustively solicits the advice of those who excel at the same activity so he can further minimize his risk. This seems like a great thing to do—to seek out best practices from others—but sometimes you've got to act and there isn't time to get feedback. When this happens, Michael tends to shut down and retreated into his shell. He gets embarrassed just anticipating how he will look if he fails."

"It sounds like Michael has some classic perfectionist attributes."

"What do you recommend I do to help him?" Alex questioned.

"Maybe he could try something he has never done before—something where failure is an unavoidable part of the process. Has he ever tried to learn a language or an instrument?"

"Nope. He has purposely avoided both activities—probably for that very reason," he reflected.

"Well, perhaps you could encourage him to branch out, though be sure to give him space to own the decision. It can be an intimidating prospect to venture out into the uncharted territory of trial and error, and that's what learning a new skill takes."

"As long as he doesn't choose the violin—I don't think I could handle the screeching!"

Conventional Approach

"I think we've talked long enough about the reasons why people fall into the Change Trap," Victoria said, "and especially about why procrastination can kill our transformation and growth. Let's take a look now at the conventional approach versus the epiphany break-through, so you can use the more effective approach without delay.

"From my experience, people only change when their pain has passed a certain threshold of tolerance or they have hit rock bottom. This is not the ideal way to confront the problems or bad habits we need to kick. It means we start making changes because of the *force of circumstance* rather than the *force of conscience*. In this scenario, people are going to live with and go through a lot of pain before making a positive change, if they ever do. Then there's the tendency to slip back into old behavior patterns once the pain is lessened to any degree—or to rely on sheer willpower to enforce change. And that is not a sustainable, long-term solution."

Epiphany Breakthrough

"Alex, the epiphany breakthrough approach is altogether different. It suggests that we enact change in our life when our conscience enlightens us. Force of conscience motivates us, not force of circumstance.

"Our conscience is like an internal GPS. It helps us know where we are, where we're heading, and the best way to get there. It can even warn us of roadblocks ahead, and how to avoid them. By proactively choosing to change now, we avoid the negative fallout of missed opportunities and bad habits run amok.

"Think about it this way: Should you wait to watch your cholesterol until you have a heart attack and need triple bypass surgery? Or should you follow a healthy eating and exercise regime to prevent this situation altogether? The answer seems so obvious in that example, but how many of us really take the steps to change before we actually have to?

"Trusting your conscience requires a leap of faith, because you are making the changes in your life before it is blatantly clear that you need to change. In life we have two choices: either we act on things or let things act upon us. When we procrastinate the changes we know we need to make, we are in essence saying: *Life, act upon me.* Conversely, when we act upon the changes we feel inspired to make (through our conscience) or are compelled to make (because of our circumstance) we are in essence saying: *Life, I'm acting on you.* So, will we act or be acted upon? The choice is ours."

Alex and Victoria sat in silence for a moment, thinking through the implications. Alex looked down at his notes.

Trap 4: The Change Trap

Why?

1. Change is difficult. It can be painful and uncomfortable.
2. We are tempted to postpone change for as long as we can.
3. As perfectionists, we live by the mantra: "If I can't be perfect, I might as well not try."

Conventional Approach

1. Change only when circumstances force you to.
2. Delay change until reaching rock bottom.
3. Rely on willpower to sustain change.

Epiphany Breakthrough

Change courageously when my conscience dictates, instead of changing when circumstances force me to.

"It looks like I've got my work cut out for me once again, Victoria," Alex declared. "I may not be a perfectionist, but I certainly put off uncomfortable change as long as I can. I wonder what my conscience will have to say about that, now that you've introduced us to one another. I can see we'll need to get better acquainted in the days ahead if I'm ever going to sort out this messy life of mine," he said with a shake of his head. "By the way, how many more traps are there?"

"Let's not get ahead of ourselves, Alex. One trap at a time will do just fine."

They decided they would meet again in two days, before Victoria headed home to Hawaii. Before he left, Alex thanked her for the delicious dinner.

* * *

Alex drove home, a bit daunted but with renewed determination. He stroked the soft leather steering wheel of his convertible as if it were a small kitten. He realized that it was time to for him to stop procrastinating and begin to focus on positive change. He knew what he needed to do—turn in this extravagant luxury sports car of his. This very purchase had started the whole chain reaction that led to Kim's abrupt departure. Although he loved driving it, he couldn't justify keeping it any longer. He was dead set on getting out of debt, and eliminating this car payment would go a long way toward that goal.

He decided he would take the car back on Saturday, when he would be free from work distractions. He dreaded facing the salesperson and the sales manager who had sold him the car. What would he say to them? How was he going to explain himself? He didn't want to think about it. He just had to act.

Saturday morning arrived and Alex drove his beloved vehicle for the last time, back to the dealership. The same men who had treated him like a king just six months ago barely even acknowledged his presence. They were clearly disappointed and tried to get Alex to change his mind—but he was fixed in his determination.

After wrangling for two hours over the buyback price, the process was complete, and the car was officially no longer his. He had sacrificed about 15 percent of its value, even though it was only six months old. Alex felt relieved but also a bit traumatized by the whole process. He walked away with enough cash to pay off his car loan, but he had lost the down payment.

The next day, Alex searched the classifieds for his next set of wheels. After an exhaustive search, he made a decision and paid the seller in cash. He was the proud new owner of an old beige compact car—complete with chipped paint, rusty door handles, and a wheezing engine. As he pressed the acceleration he no longer heard the powerful purr he was used to. Instead it made more of a hiss. He turned up the radio to drown out the pitiful noise.

Had he honestly traded his luxury convertible for this sad excuse of a vehicle? Alex's ego felt bruised and battered, but there was no doubt that a burden had been lifted as well. His conscience was free for the first time in a long time. He knew somehow that the sacrifice would be worth it.

What would Chaz think? Surprisingly, Alex found that he didn't care what Chaz thought. What would his kids think? They might actually be impressed. He had finally followed through on what he knew he needed to do. And for that he felt very proud. What would Kim think? His thoughts trailed off, as he realized how much he missed her input and companionship.

Alex pulled into his driveway in his old clunker and saw Laura looking out the window at him with a confused look on her face.

"Ummm . . . what happened to your convertible? Is it at the repair shop?" Laura queried.

"Oh, no, actually. I turned it back into the dealership yesterday." Alex said with a huge grin, sensing Laura's embarrassment.

"But I told my friends we could take your car out tonight. Now what am I going to do?"

"You can take my new car if you want," said Alex, jingling the keys in front of her face.

"Seriously Dad, you've got to be kidding me! Why did you have to do that? You've ruined everything!" Laura whined.

"I'm sorry, Laura. I didn't know you had plans with your friends to use my car," he replied.

"How was I supposed to know you were going to ditch your car out of the blue?" Laura asked.

"You couldn't have. But I've been thinking about taking the car back for quite some time," Alex admitted.

"Is this because we're so broke?" Laura pressed resentfully.

"Yes! That, and how upset my purchase of the car made your mother. My conscience has been working on me to do this. It's the right thing to do right now," Alex explained. "Plus, I really want to start putting some money away for your college expenses."

"Really?" Laura was caught off guard. "I didn't think you even cared."

"Of course I do. A great deal. I'd rather be setting aside money for you than making a luxury car payment, as enjoyable as that beauty of a car was for me to drive," Alex told her.

"I thought my college plans were being cast aside with everything else happening to us right now," Laura said.

"Not true. We just haven't taken the time to talk about it yet," said Alex. "Would you like to take a few minutes right now?"

"Sure, if you're not too busy driving that thing around!" Laura teased.

Alex and Laura ended up talking together for the next hour, discussing Laura's college plans and dreams. She was really torn about whether she should go to college directly out of high school or spend a year exploring, working, and traveling before she jumped headlong into such a big commitment. She could see the benefit of both options, but was unsure what to do. Alex listened and advised her the best he knew how.

In the end, Laura decided that she would take a break for one year before starting college, but would prepare for and take the SAT exam before she graduated high school, while she was still in an academic mode. Alex commended Laura for her decision and offered his support.

Laura also shared her fear that she might not have what it takes to be successful in college. She admitted that she had a hard time changing her undisciplined habits (skipping school and avoiding her studies), but she found her father's recent changes inspiring. If he could muster the courage to change from a convertible to an economy car, maybe she could make the changes she needed to in her own life.

The front door slammed as Michael walked in from soccer practice and tossed his sports bag in the corner. "Hey Dad, what's with the beige car in our driveway? Where'd your other car go?"

"You'll never believe it," Alex smiled.

Later that evening, Alex overheard Michael talking with his mom on the phone. He guessed Michael was telling Kim of the latest chapter in his father's transformation. He wondered if it would make a difference to her, perhaps aid in their reconciliation somehow. He had to hope.

Back at work, Alex's momentum continued. He decided on a number of things he was going to do differently, in order to escape the Focus Trap. The first thing was to no longer keep his schedule so open. Up until now, anyone could schedule an appointment with him at will. From now on, if they wanted an appointment they'd have to request it from Alex's assistant, and the request would need to be clear and specific—no more open-ended meetings. He'd also curbed the drop-by visits from Chaz and others, which would begin innocently enough but extend to hours of unproductive banter.

The second change Alex made was to block out time in his calendar for planning and thinking. Now that was new! This had been something he had always avoided. But no longer. Now that he was taking control of his own time, he became amazed at all of the open space in his schedule.

The third change Alex planned to enact was to say no to any nonessential meetings. For every week during the prior six months, he'd only had about 10 unscheduled hours out of the 50 hours he spent at the office each week. Scheduled meetings had consumed 40 hours of each week! Half of those meetings directly involved his peers, and the other half involved presentations by other people who directly reported to him. His goal over the next year was to cut these meetings in half, down to 20 hours a week, and the year following that, down to 10 hours a week. Alex knew this would be a difficult change, and one he would have to get his boss to agree to, but he was determined to make it work to increase his productivity.

As he started to make these changes at work, two things surprised him: one, the number of thin things he had been mired in, and two, how resistant other people were to his desired changes.

He was mulling over how to present this plan to his boss when he received a text from Kim. He nearly dropped his phone in his eagerness to open it and respond. The text contained a snapshot of his new set of used wheels, probably sent to her by Michael. Beneath the photo was simply a question mark. This was the first time Kim had reached out to him about anything other than the kids since that disastrous day back in April when she had left. Alex was tempted to dive in with an in-depth explanation, but a text didn't feel like the right medium for such an important conversation. He simply responded with an exclamation point. A few moments later, she sent back a smiley face.

Alex leaned back and exhaled deeply. Now, this was a definite improvement from the impassable wall Kim had put up since she left. It still stung to think about the weekend in May, when she had driven down to spend time with their kids but had refused to see him. Their only communication had been through their children, mostly Michael for that matter. He found himself hoping that this gesture would open the door to further communication and a bridging of the chasm that had grown between them over the past . . . who knew how long?

Alex's thoughts came back to his work. He had discovered that the people who directly reported to him were not the least bit disappointed by his efforts to reduce the number of meetings—in fact, they seemed happy and appreciative. He copied out Parkinson's law onto a sign he made then posted on his desk: "Work expands itself to the amount of time allotted." He was beginning to appreciate the truth of it. He negotiated with the organizer of a meeting to which he contributed to reduce his participation from weekly to twice a month. She was not happy, but she agreed to postpone any Alex-relevant issues to the times when he would be in attendance.

The change that elicited the most resistance was the closing off of his schedule to anyone and everyone. His assistant still had requests for upwards of 20 hours a week of Alex's time. But he'd only approved five hours a week—a 75 percent reduction. Half of the requests, it seemed, involved problems that legitimately belonged to others. He was good at getting things done and delegating responsibility, and that attracted people who wanted him to get *their* projects done as well. Without Alex's help, they had to find other people to solve their problems, or they had to solve those problems themselves. There were growing pains all around.

Interestingly enough, one of the people who was most vocally resistant to the change in Alex's schedule was Chaz. Alex figured that on average Chaz and his team had taken up about 10 hours of his week. Because Chaz's team did not directly report to Alex, he cut all of this time out. Before long, Chaz confronted him.

"What's up?" Alex inquired innocently, as Chaz stormed into his office.

"We need to talk," Chaz blustered.

Alex had been arriving at work early and parking at the rear of the building so that Chaz wouldn't know he had sold his car. He wasn't quite ready to tell him yet. And he'd learned from sad experience that eating out with Chaz meant that he would inevitably be left to pick up the bill.

"I don't know if today's a good day for me to meet. Sorry Chaz."

A hurt look passed across Chaz's face. "What's happened to you, dude? My team and I can't even get on your schedule. You used to have my back. I thought I could depend on you."

Alex was starting to recognize how very one-sided their relation-ship had always been. "I've eliminated all meetings with you and your direct reports," Alex said firmly.

"But why? We generated such magic when we would all get together!"

"Those meetings were spent resolving *your* team's issues, and I just don't want you to miss those powerful opportunities to mentor your own people."

"But, you have such a fresh take, Alex. We need you. I need you. Now everyone is coming to me for all the answers," Chaz lamented.

"And you're the right guy for the job, Chaz! In fact, that *is* your job." Alex smiled encouragingly.

"I thought you were my friend, man," Chaz muttered as he backed out the doorway, shaking his head in a daze.

If Chaz had been honest with himself, he wouldn't have faulted Alex for making the change. What bothered Chaz the most was that now his gig was up. Alex, his favorite go-to problem solver, wasn't making himself available to solve his problems anymore. He'd have to shoulder his own burdens from here on out. No more free ride. Chaz kicked a wastebasket on the way back to his office, sending it reeling down the hall.

Alex smiled to himself as Chaz disappeared from view. He felt like he'd won a personal victory—he'd liberated himself from the agendas of others that he had so readily shouldered in the past. Of course he was ready to help a friend in need, but he wasn't going to be taken advantage of like he unwittingly had been. Chaz wasn't the only one who was unhappy with the changes Alex had made, but Alex himself couldn't have been happier!

In the past Alex had justified his problem solving for coworkers by saying that his job was geared to executing the agenda of his boss. But now Alex realized that he had helped facilitate the codependency that had occurred throughout the majority of his career.

Alex's efforts to spend more time planning proved to be very beneficial. He started working *on* the business, not just *in* the business. He found new ways to generate revenue and noticed the time- and revenue-wasting mistakes that his team repeatedly made. He discarded sales approaches that generated minimal success but had endured as part of the historical legacy of the company. In their stead, he found that he was open to fresh ideas and new ways of thinking.

Alex remembered the powerful waves that had knocked him over in Hawaii, when he had felt he might drown as the forces of nature thrust him effortlessly under the weight of the sea. In the same way, he was finally emerging from crisis management mode, where he'd been simply trying to stay afloat as each new problem came crashing over him. He felt buoyant now. He could navigate the ebb and flow of the work at hand with a feeling of control and clarity of vision. The sense of panic that had been a way of life until recently had been replaced by his renewed sense of purpose.

Alex also felt he could stand apart from the business, as if he were an objective observer, gathering insights and impressions for the next strategy he could implement. Prior to this, he had been implementing someone else's strategy. Now he felt empowered, in alignment with his boss but capable of placing his own unique stamp on the business. In the past, Alex had shown competent management skills but lacked visionary leadership. Now he was exhibiting both characteristics.

One of the things Alex still struggled with was learning how to say no without feeling guilty. He was thrilled with the results of his new approach but sometimes fell back into the mode of trying to please others. He realized that the desire to please others could be a kind of trap in and of itself. Sure, it came with the immediate short-term reward of thanks and praise, and the satisfaction gained from pleasing his boss or the person making the request, but the consequences of taking on too much and being stretched too thin ended up taking its toll as he couldn't accomplish everything he had committed to do. There was definitely a learning curve to this new way of life, but he felt encouraged that he was moving in the right direction.

Alex learned that he couldn't run farther or faster than his strength would allow. He couldn't do it all—and that was okay. It was a hard but enormously freeing lesson to learn. He also began to examine his priorities—what mattered most to him. Many of the things that had occupied his time and attention in the past seemed far less important to him now. Golfing two rounds with his friends on Saturday was fun and relaxing, but it took up his whole day. Did he have an equivalent amount of time allocated for his wife and kids? If he had, he imagined that Kim would now be by his side instead of distant and estranged.

He had also missed many of Michael's soccer games because of his golf outings. He vowed he would not miss them anymore. Plus, Alex now realized that his friends had just been leeching off of him. When Alex said they should find another place to golf other than his country club—where he ended up paying for everyone on his account— suddenly golfing become a low priority for them. No one else stepped up and volunteered to host or pay—not even once. It was eye-opening, to say the least.

When he took a closer look at his life, Alex realized how obsessed he'd been with watching sporting events on television. He'd probably been watching 20 hours of sports each week: Sunday night football, Monday night football, Thursday and Friday night college football, Saturday football (if he wasn't busy golfing), and of course Sunday football. And once football was over, basketball took its place, and then hockey and baseball. It was all very enjoyable, but was it really necessary and important to watch that much television every week throughout the whole year?

Because Alex was in a reflective mood, he wondered why it had taken him so long to start making these changes in his life. Having Kim move out of the house was a huge blow to his ego, but why had he procrastinated dealing with the obvious for so long? And why did it take the observations of an old friend for him to gain perspective, when his wife had been there all along saying the same thing? *Timing is everything, I guess*, he sighed to himself. He just hadn't been ready to face the truth that had been staring him in the face for so long. At least now he was headed in the right direction.

Trap 5: The Learning Trap

Two days breezed by and Alex once again found himself on Victoria's hotel balcony, perusing the room service dinner menu. He decided to go with the Caesar salad this time. A light meal would balance the potentially heavy discussion to come. He was sure she would illuminate the additional traps he had fallen into, and he felt a sense of anticipation.

"Alex, of all the traps we've talked about, I'm most excited to discuss this one with you," Victoria said.

"Uh oh, I'm getting nervous."

"Hush, my young apprentice," she replied. "The fifth trap is the Learning Trap, and its big theme is: mistakes—why we've got it all wrong."

"All right, you've got me. I'm intrigued," Alex pulled the cap off his pen to start taking notes.

"From my observation and experience, there are several reasons why we fall into the Learning Trap." Victoria took a deep breath. "First, it is much easier to hide our mistakes than it is to be accountable for them. We see them as character flaws—or defects, rather than part of the learning process. We have a persona that we want to project—this persona becomes damaged and tainted when others see our mistakes—and we will do everything within our power to keep this image pristine. We shouldn't forget that mistakes are an essential part of our life's journey."

Hiding or Spinning Mistakes

"Our instinctual reaction when we make a mistake is to hide it. Let's look into this a little further," Victoria continued.

"Please," Alex said.

"If I'm able to hide my mistakes from others, I've succeeded in maintaining a particular image. The problem with this approach is that by hiding my mistake, I can't learn from it. What's more, it requires a lot of effort to hide. This effort is better spent on reflection and insight that can lead to a course correction and growth.

"Now, I'm not a big fan of politics, but there is an extremely valuable lesson regarding President Richard Nixon's resignation in the mid-1970s that relates to this trap. You and Bobby were just toddlers at that time." Victoria paused and smiled whenever she mentioned Bobby.

"President Nixon wasn't forced to resign because of the Watergate break-in. He was forced to resign because of the Watergate *cover-up*. Isn't that interesting? Rather than acknowledge his mistake, Nixon dragged the country through two years of misery until the evidence was brought forth, confirming the truth that Nixon had been hiding all along. He might have been forgiven for the Watergate break-in had he confessed when the story broke, but he couldn't be forgiven for the elaborate, arrogant cover-up he initiated," she explained.

"It was also revealing to learn about Nixon's beliefs about the choices he made as president. When David Frost interviewed Nixon in 1977, he asked him whether it was okay for him as president to do something illegal. Nixon replied: *When the president does it, that means that it is not illegal.* President Nixon thought that he was above the law! From Nixon's perspective, because he was president, there was nothing wrong with the break-in, and therefore nothing wrong with the cover-up.

"But sometimes we don't hide our mistakes—we just spin them," Victoria pointed out. "Spinning is equivalent to rewriting, rationalizing, and justifying—and President Nixon did just that.

"By spinning, we reassign the blame from us to others rather than taking personal responsibility and accountability. We see these spin masters weaving their smooth-talking, silver-tongued rhetoric in all arenas of life—politics, law, business, academia, religion, and society at large.

"If we can successfully transfer the blame from ourselves to others, we will have succeeded in remaining mistake free. The other option is to label the mistake as an anomaly, a one-off or an unusual occurrence that is unlikely to happen again. In this way, we justify and rationalize away our part, or we diminish our role so that we are painted in a more favorable light."

Mistakes Are Seen as Character Flaws

"The second reason we fall into the Learning Trap is because we see our mistakes as character flaws. When we repeatedly make the same mistakes over and over again, it becomes hard to visualize ourselves in a different light. We begin to feel that our mistakes, and especially our repeated mistakes, define us. They seem to determine who we are—

tainted and imperfect. But, of course, this is an inaccurate way for us to define ourselves. We are not merely the sum of our past choices—but are infinitely more capable with limitless possibilities ahead of us. The past, even the most recent past, is history."

Alex nodded hopefully to Victoria, encouraged by the notion that he could create a new reality.

"Don't be too hard on yourself, okay? This is a challenging transformation you are undertaking; it is especially difficult because our modern world pressures us into thinking that we are defined by our mistakes. Most of the time, we are our own worst critics," Victoria reassured.

We Protect Our Persona

Victoria cleared her throat. "The third reason our approach to making mistakes allows us to fall into the Learning Trap involves trying to protect our image from the outside world—our family, friends, work associates, neighbors, and so on. People often refer to this as our public persona.

"It's almost as if preserving our positive self-image is hardwired into our brains. I think that's why spinning mistakes or pushing the blame onto someone else is such a common instinctive reaction. If we publicly reveal our struggles, or worse, make mistakes of all shapes and sizes, we face the fear that we won't be held in high esteem by others."

Victoria's words made Alex think back on his work environment over the years. When he was a sales manager and he'd had a bad day, he always tried to slip out of the office without having to interact or explain it to anyone. Even when he got home, he didn't want to confide in Kim. The pressure to perform every day was a burden, but he simply had to toe the line. After all, he was a sales manager and his team looked up to him. No excuses could be made.

Victoria continued, "Social pressure to portray a positive—often unrealistic—self-image is high. And when we don't live up to that ideal standard, we lose faith in ourselves.

"Today, more than ever, we're looking for role models who project and portray what we find lacking in ourselves. We hold these people up as our ideal. But, alas, even our role models fall short of the pedestal we put them on.

"There's a risk to admitting and owning up to our mistakes: we become ordinary. We all like to think of ourselves as being above the cut, one of a kind, unique in some special way. If we are forced to admit that we aren't all that anymore, then we feel just plain average, and no one likes to feel that way. We will do anything to avoid looking and feeling average. If you're anything like me, you can relate to what I'm talking about . . ." Victoria's voice trailed off for a moment as she looked at the city lights twinkling below.

Conventional Approach

"When we make mistakes and struggle to attain the image of what we're striving for, the conventional approach suggests we try something else, or do something we can succeed at. 'Everyone has a talent for doing something great—what's yours?' You know what I mean?" Victoria asked.

"Completely," Alex responded. "I remember in junior high how Bobby was such a natural at skateboarding. There wasn't anything he couldn't do—almost instantly, too." Victoria smiled in agreement. "I tried hard to skateboard at first, but I didn't pick it up as easily as he did, so I acted like I didn't care about it. Bobby just learned so quickly! So I decided to take on basketball instead. I wonder if he ever was on to me," said Alex, lost in the memory.

Victoria shrugged. "The problem with this solution of skipping to whatever comes easiest is that it shortchanges the natural process of growth and progression. We assume that gifted people, or geniuses as we might label them, are immune to this natural process. But they're not. We all must go through it. Are you familiar with Malcolm Gladwell's 10,000-hour rule?"

Alex replied, "Isn't that the concept that a person can master anything by devoting 10,000 hours to that particular subject?"[1]

"Exactly. The two examples I like best from Gladwell's book, *Outliers*, are from the lives of Wolfgang Amadeus Mozart and the Beatles. In both cases, most people incorrectly assume that these musicians were naturally gifted, and didn't have to work very hard to develop their talents. But upon closer inspection, a different picture emerges. In Mozart's case, although he was writing music at age six, his greatest concertos occurred later in his life. He simply logged his 10,000 hours much earlier than most people, by age 21. But he put in those 10,000 hours nevertheless."

"Regarding the Beatles—"

"I love the Beatles," Alex grinned.

"Who doesn't? Rob and I remember them bursting onto the American music scene when they performed on the *Ed Sullivan Show* in February 1964, and we assumed they were born musical geniuses. But, similar to Mozart's case, the Beatles performed live about 1,200 times before they had their big break.[2] Most bands don't perform that many times in their entire career. The Beatles put in the practice time to achieve such widespread success; it wasn't just an innate gift."

"Hang on," Alex interrupted. "You're suggesting that Mozart and the Beatles succeeded simply because of hard work? They were also very talented."

"That's not quite what I'm saying, but I'll touch on that again in a minute, okay?" Victoria said.

"All right," Alex shrugged.

Epiphany Breakthrough

"Alex, the epiphany breakthrough for the Learning Trap requires that we take stock of the process, not just the results. The effort it takes to get there is equally as important as the actual results. Society today is obsessed with the end result, while discounting and minimizing the effort it takes to produce it.

Let's go back to the image of toddlers learning to walk. Can you imagine if the parent of those toddlers only rewarded and praised them if they succeeded in walking the first time they tried? And yet that is exactly how we treat most people. We only offer our praise if we like the outcome; we rarely celebrate the effort, the journey, the progress, or the improvement.

"You also see this in athletics. Seldom is the effort in training praised and acknowledged as much as a win. Praise and acknowledgment are only offered with the win—the right outcome—the positive end result. And yet consistent results or progress will never be achieved without effort—the diligent and consistent work that goes into creating success. And that effort involves more than a few mistakes along the way," Victoria elaborated.

In a slightly irritated tone Alex responded, "I think I'm missing what's so wrong with celebrating victory. No one praises athletes for practicing if they don't win, and that's socially acceptable. What counts is what happens on the court or field of play. I don't think I agree with what you're saying. From my experience, I've seen that praising results *yields results*. If my team doesn't hit the sales goal, for instance, I'm not going to congratulate them with a big ol' pat on the back, you know?" Alex folded his arms.

Victoria looked concerned. "I think that's a limited worldview to live by, Alex, but I can't force you to see things another way." She exhaled deeply. "At least just let me finish my explanation and then you may conclude what you will from there. Okay?"

"Sure," Alex said curtly. Victoria was way off on this one. She must not have any experience in the athletic or professional world, he thought.

"Okay. Well, a few years ago I read a book by the psychologist Carol Dweck and it completely rocked my world. She studied and wrote about the importance of praising *efforts* when raising children. I actually brought her book to read a few of my favorite insights to you. May I?" she asked.

Alex heaved a sigh. "Sure. Go ahead."

Victoria pulled the book from her suitcase and thumbed through its pages. There wasn't a page on which she hadn't underlined something.

"Great. Here it is." She cleared her throat before beginning:

After seven experiments with hundreds of children, we had some of the clearest findings I've ever seen: Praising children's intelligence harms their motivation and it harms their performance. How can that be? Don't children love to be praised? Yes, children love praise. And they especially love to be praised for their intelligence and talent. It really does give them a boost, a special glow—but only for the moment. The minute they hit a snag, their confidence goes out the window and their motivation hits rock bottom. If success means they're smart, then failure means they're dumb. That's the fixed mindset.[3]

She searched the pages. "Ah, this one's great, too." She continued:

Parents think they can hand children permanent confidence—like a gift—by praising their brains and talent. It doesn't work, and in fact has the opposite effect. It makes children doubt themselves as soon as anything is hard or anything goes wrong. If parents want to give their children a gift, the best thing they can do is to teach their children to love challenges, be intrigued by mistakes, enjoy effort, and keep on learning. That way, their children don't have to be slaves to praise. They will have a lifelong way to build and repair their own confidence.[4]

Victoria searched for the next quote and her finger landed on another line: "'No matter what your ability is,'" she read, "'effort is what ignites that ability and turns it into accomplishment.'[5] Love that one. This affirms what I was telling you about the 10,000-hour rule. The Beatles *did* have natural talent—Mozart too—but their talent would have been wasted without hard work.

"Oh! This one too!" she exclaimed. "Sorry, almost done, just lots of good stuff in here. Last one, I promise." Victoria glanced at Alex. "'John Wooden, the legendary basketball coach, says you aren't a failure until you start to blame. What he means is that you can still be in the process of learning from your mistakes until you deny them.'"[6]

"So what you're telling me is that failure is just part of the path we're walking, right?" Alex asked as he picked up his pen again.

"Even better, Alex, you don't have to view your mistakes as failure at all. Mistakes are simply part of the process. Making mistakes doesn't condemn you to failure—but by John Wooden's definition, denial and blaming does. If we acknowledge and learn from our mistakes instead of spinning them, we're not sidelined from reaching our vision—we are *enabled*!" Victoria said with conviction.

"As a human race, we need a paradigm shift regarding how we view our own mistakes as well as the mistakes of others. But we tend to judge ourselves by our intentions—by what we meant to do. We tend to judge others by their behaviors—by what we see them do. It would be difficult to guess another's intentions, wouldn't it? Having a more generous mindset, by affording others the same amount of slack we allow ourselves helps us to adopt this new perspective," she added.

Alex was busily taking notes. At first, he had doubted the information Victoria was feeding him, but the quotes from Dr. Dweck had really changed his perspective.

"Could I see that book?" he asked, with his hand extended.

"I dog-eared the pages I quoted," Victoria remarked as she passed the book to Alex's outstretched hand.

Alex was realizing how far off the mark he'd been raising his children and mentoring his sales associates. He had never praised effort before. It was almost as if praise was scarce, and he couldn't use his approval to award anything but successful results. He was definitely guilty of heaping too much praise on both kids over particular outcomes rather than effort demonstrated. But that was about to change.

"Watching you take notes like that leads me to think you enjoyed our conversation," Victoria guessed. Alex jokingly covered his notes with his hand.

"No evidence of that yet," he retorted, "but actually, yeah. You've once again opened my mind."

Victoria beamed. "Well then, there is another insight I want to share with you. I think it may help you transition from where you are to where you want to go in relation to the Learning Trap."

"Hit me with it," Alex surrendered.

"Okay, then, no more making fun of me. Got it?" she pointed her finger menacingly.

Alex smiled and held his hands up as if at gunpoint. She laughed.

"Well as you know, I'm a big proponent of energy and energy flow, and I've long admired the work of the psychologist Jim Loehr. In one of my favorite books of his, he writes about the stories—or the narrative—we tell ourselves. He says 'a story is our creation of reality; indeed, our story matters *more* than what actually happens. By "story," then I mean those tales we create and tell ourselves and others, and which *form the only reality we will ever know in this life*.'[7]

"Anytime you are trying to make drastic changes—like what you are currently doing, Alex—you need to start creating in your mind the *new story*, while at the same time silencing the *old story* that is ingrained in your head," Victoria explained.

"Okay, keep going," Alex said.

"If you continue to believe the same old narrative—Alex's Old Story—your behaviors will inevitably follow and the changes you seek won't gain any traction.

"Conversely, if the story in your head represents a new narrative—Alex's Trap-Free Story—then the desired new behaviors will come to fruition."

"I really like what you're saying." Alex hesitated. "But it's not like Old-Story Alex will just surrender to a new narrative. I mean, I've been this way my whole life. What you're saying is encouraging, but I just don't see it as entirely possible."

Victoria smiled. She was so fond of Alex. He was bold and afraid, strong and insecure all at once. She could read that he longed for transformation, but doubted his own ability to achieve it.

"Alex," she said warmly, "You can't cling to your old story. Until you change the narrative in your head, you cannot expect the behaviors to follow. I know you can do this!"

Victoria's belief in Alex made him feel for a moment that he could become New-Story Alex. He managed a smile. "Thank you, Victoria. That means a lot to me."

"In his book Loehr suggests taking two key steps to accomplish this. The first is to quiet the internal chatter and the second is to summon your inner voice.[8] And, like anything new, this requires practice to fully develop. This is one of the revolutionary, unconventional insights in making lasting change," Victoria explained.

"I get it. I didn't realize how much my old story narrative has been playing out in my head. I can see now how it's been impeding my progress," he confessed. "Every time I start to move forward, the old story narrative tries to derail me, and doubt creeps back in. Now that I understand the forces at play, I will try to nip that inaccurate narrative in the bud and replace it with my new story narrative." Alex appeared visibly relieved by this insight, and by his ability to articulate it to Victoria.

"Nice summary, Alex. You're definitely a quick learner." Victoria continued. "Our progress as humans is dependent upon our ability to learn and grow from the mistakes we make in this life. We teach and believe this when we are young—as a toddler or child or a young adult. But somehow along the way, we have lost sight of this principle as adults. Somehow, we've created this world where we expect ourselves and others to be practically perfect, but this isn't realistic or healthy.

"Life's experiences enable us to develop, progress, and advance. When we attempt to deny our mistakes or spin them instead of learning from them, we stunt our growth, making us stagnant and subject to making these same mistakes again and again," Victoria summarized.

Alex looked down at his watch. Once again, more than three hours had passed. Previously he had been impressed by Victoria and her insights, but their discussion today on the Learning Trap had been mind-bending. He knew where he'd gone wrong in the past, but now was he was able to see his mistakes in a new light. It was all part of his progress—he could now begin to learn from his mistakes. This felt like a total game changer. It wasn't just an exercise to accomplish; the Learning Trap was about redefining how he thought about life, *his* life.

For as long as he could remember, Alex had been all about denial or self-sabotage when it came to confronting his mistakes. He realized that by understanding how this trap applied to him, he had given himself a whole new perspective on life. This was a breakthrough for Alex.

"Victoria, this has been so insightful. I can't thank you enough. I'm excited to apply these learnings in my life. I like how you've framed them for me," he remarked.

"This has been a transformative experience for me as well, Alex. You've been like a sponge, taking in all that I've had to say. Your willingness to examine and make changes in your life is unusual and inspiring. I look forward to our future conversations."

"So do I," Alex said. "I hope you had a wonderful time at the conference, Victoria. Are you excited to get back to Rob and the beach house?"

"It was a fantastic conference, but yes, it will be great to be back home," she replied, giving him a goodbye hug.

They agreed to meet up in another couple months, this time via videoconference. Then Alex was on his way. On the elevator down to the parking garage, he opened his Trap Journal and looked at what he had written.

Trap 5: The Learning Trap

Why?

1. We don't take accountability for our choices. We hide our mistakes and rewrite our biographies instead of owning up to them.
2. We see our mistakes as character defects, rather than part of the learning journey.
3. We have a persona that we try to project to others. It becomes damaged and tainted when others see our flaws. We instinctively try to protect this image.

Conventional Approach

If you aren't good at it, try something else. If you can't get the desired results quickly, do something that yields better results before someone notices you are failing.

Epiphany Breakthrough

Rejoice and celebrate in the effort, the journey, and the process as much as in the end result. Mistakes are instructive. Learn from them instead of hiding them.

Alex was excited to implement some new responses to past and future mistakes, just as the Learning Trap revealed.

* * *

Now that Alex was golfing much less than before, he began to attend Michael's soccer games during the week as well as on weekends. Michael played forward on his club team. Alex hadn't realized just how intense Michael was when it came to competing in his chosen sport.

Toward the end of one of his games, Michael missed converting a few key shots into goals, and his coach put him on the bench. Michael was fuming. His team ended up losing the game by one goal. Alex tried to console his son after the game, but Michael wouldn't have any of it. Finally, a few minutes into their drive home, Michael blurted out:

"Can you believe how pathetic I played?"

"Actually, I thought you played pretty well. You nearly scored five goals. Their goalie did a great job defending. We must have had 20 shots on goal."

"Yeah, and we only made two of them—it's pathetic!" Michael lamented.

"But you have to credit their goalie. Our goalie gave up three goals on eight or nine shots on goal. He simply didn't defend as well as their goalie did," Alex countered.

"Had I made one single goal, we would have sent the game into overtime with penalty kicks. If I had made two more goals, we would have won the game. I can't believe I didn't make it happen," Michael ranted.

"Michael, listen to me. You played very well. The other team was just a little more on their game today, and I attribute most of their win to their goalie."

Michael wasn't listening. "Maybe I shouldn't play forward anymore. Maybe I shouldn't play soccer anymore! If I can't deliver for the team when they need me most, then I have no business being on the team," he concluded angrily. "Coach was right in taking me out. He knows that in the end, I choke when the game is on the line."

Alex couldn't believe what he was hearing. He knew his son had high standards, but to put this whole loss on his own shoulders was taking it too far. Alex realized he'd contributed indirectly to Michael's response, because in the past he himself had focused heavily on results—whether the game was a win or a loss. Alex had offered little or no affirmation on the process, or encouragement toward the growth and learning his son was experiencing, even through missed shots and lost games.

In times past, when Michael came home from his soccer games, Alex asked only two questions: "Did you win?" and "How many goals did you score?" When Michael answered, "We lost," Alex would respond, "That totally stinks." And if Michael didn't score any goals, Alex would say, "Well, that's too bad." He never asked about Michael's progress, or the skills he was working on. It had always been about the end result.

"I want you to know that I'm proud of you and all of the progress you're making," Alex said as they pulled into the driveway.

"Yeah, right, like you've ever cared about my progress," Michael yelled. He slammed the car door shut and stormed off to his room.

"What's up with Michael?" Laura asked.

"He lost his game," Alex responded.

"What was the score?"

"3–2."

"Did Michael score any goals?"

"No," said Alex.

"Oh, that stinks!" said Laura.

The irony of the situation did not escape Alex.

A couple hours later, when Michael had cooled off a little, Alex decided it was a good time to have a talk about what had happened at the game.

Alex knocked on his door. "Hey, do you have a minute?"

"Yeah, sure, what's goin' on?" Michael seemed to have perked up.

"I want to apologize for not being very supportive of your soccer in the past. I didn't make it to hardly any of your games. I've also realized I only ever asked about the results instead of listening to you about what you were finding most challenging, what you were learning, and what you were experiencing. I want to change that going forward," Alex said softly.

"Yeah, it seemed weird that you were suddenly interested in anything but the win. So why do you care now?" Michael asked.

"Because I realize I've put hardly any emphasis on celebrating the effort you've put in and the progress you've made. I want to hear more about your goals with soccer, and how I can support you in reaching them."

"You are becoming an enlightened old man, Pa!" Michael quipped.

"Well, I'm not there yet, son. Certainly not where I want to be. But I hope I'm headed in the right direction. And I can't take credit for this insight. Victoria told me about an enlightening study on parenting that describes how parents nowadays heap praise upon their kids for results but fail to celebrate the progress and growth that comes through failure as well as success. Celebrating the process is key, because when there are the inevitable struggles in life, kids start to label themselves as unsuccessful because they're struggling. Yet it's in the struggle that the learning and growth occur," Alex elaborated.

"Sounds interesting," said Michael.

"So Michael, when you said you were thinking about quitting soccer because you couldn't deliver the win for your team, you were saying that because you've been conditioned to believe that success is directly connected with winning, and by default, failure is directly connected with losing. But that is not how life works. None of us can win all the time. Even the best teams don't win all the time. In fact, it usually takes a whole lot of losses to finally get to any winning season."

Michael nodded in agreement.

"As your father, I want to help you focus more on the process, and on *your* progress. I know it'll be a new operating mode, and it might take some practice to get it right. I know I've passed the results-focused mindset onto you because that's how I was raised. But now I see how unhelpful that's been for you. Never give up on your goals and your passion, Michael, because of the occasional setback. You can use those apparent stumbling blocks as stepping stones to take you closer to where you want to be.

"Victoria has taught me something else, too. Conventional wisdom dictates that if we don't always excel at something, then we should do something else that comes easier. In other words, don't let others see your weakness; distance yourself from any mistake through blame or denial. The epiphany breakthrough suggests we look at mistakes and struggles as an essential part of life's journey; they are instructive and help us move forward. They are not a reason to quit and do something else that comes more easily," explained Alex.

"But, I can't stand it when I don't do something just right," Michael insisted.

"I know, Michael. That's because you have some perfectionist tendencies. You live by the philosophy, *if I can't do it perfectly, I might as well not try.*"

"That's a philosophy?" Michael asked.

"Very much so," Alex confirmed. "Your challenge is that you're a perfectionist. My challenge is that I have a hard time accepting and forgiving my mistakes. According to Victoria, we both have got it wrong. But we are in good company. Much of our modern world operates on this flawed basis."

Alex looked somberly into Michael's eyes. "Hey, I hope you don't quit soccer because you've had a frustrating game. I think you're becoming a better player and gaining experience with each game, and the team would be much worse off without you."

"Thanks, Dad, you're right . . . I'm not going to quit soccer. I was just really disappointed by the loss and the fact that I couldn't get the ball past their dang goalie. Man, was he good! I'll try not to be so hard on myself," he said with genuine appreciation.

"As a wise master once said to his young padawan: 'Try? Try not! *Do*, or *do not*, there is no try!" Alex mimicked a Yoda voice.

Michael laughed and threw a pillow at his father. "So now you're a Jedi master, are you?"

Alex smiled as he closed the door behind him and went to make dinner.

As he was draining the pasta for the spaghetti and meatballs he was making for dinner, Alex thought about their conversation. He was grateful Michael had been so receptive and rebounded so quickly from his disappointment. Kids are resilient, he mused. It made sense to think of everyone as a work in process, including himself. By doing that, it was easier to cut everyone some slack—the same slack he hoped people would permit him.

* * *

Since the sale of his luxury car, a door had opened between Alex and Kim. Ever since then, they had been having short weekly talks to discuss issues with the kids. That was at least a start. During these calls, Alex had still been defensive around his behaviors and his role in their separation. Kim responded in kind. But on tonight's particular call, after going through the Learning Trap with Victoria, Alex was in a completely different frame of mind. Instead of feeling defensive, he'd begun to own up to the mistakes he had made over the years, especially those leading up to their separation. He recognized that the motto—"never show any weakness"—might be a perfectly good motto for a football team, but it wasn't a good motto by which to live his life.

"Kim, I've gained some amazing new insights from Victoria in our last discussion. We talked about mistakes and why, when we try to deal with them, we get it all wrong."

"Hmm. That sounds interesting. Tell me more."

"Well, she explained that we fail to realize the important role mistakes play in our life. We try to hide them or spin them instead of owning up to them and learning from them." Alex said.

"Keep talking," said Kim.

"Well, it's helped me realize how often I've tried to hide or spin my mistakes in our marriage, instead of admitting where I have fallen short."

Alex had captured Kim's full attention. "Go on," she encouraged.

"I want to apologize for the mistakes I've made that have contributed to our separation, Kim. I'm sorry. I hope you will forgive me and give us another chance," Alex said.

"This is certainly a very different stance for you," Kim remarked.

"Yeah, completely different," Alex responded.

"From what the kids tell me, Alex, you've been making some impressive changes in your habits and priorities. I hope it lasts," Kim observed skeptically.

Trap 6:
The Career Trap

Alex was excelling at work. Through applying the epiphany break-through from the Focus Trap, he was making a greater impact and providing inspirational leadership. His mind was dialed in on his most important priorities. Nevertheless, he couldn't deny an underlying sense of unease and a lack of appreciation at work.

The quality of his work had increased due to the changes he'd been making, but he still felt undervalued. Though he'd experienced more fulfillment since he'd enacted the changes to get out of the focus trap, his passion for his job had been waning for quite some time. Purpose was what Alex found most lacking in his professional life. What lasting contribution was he actually making? Working with clients was definitely his favorite part of the job, and he received very favorable reviews from them. But most of the time, his work was passionless and mundane.

Ever since he was a kid, Alex had wanted to be an entrepreneur. He didn't like being managed by a boss; he preferred to be self-directed. As he aged, this desire for independence stuck with him. His sales roles gave him some autonomy, but he mostly felt like a tool being used to give his boss and the company what they wanted most—*more sales*. He was merely a means to an end. Alex realized that being a sales manager would always be a job of short-term memory wins. It didn't matter how impressive the prior year or quarter was, it always came down to: "What are you going to do for me this month? How about this week?" Alex was annoyed by the short-term mentality of his leaders in the company.

At the start of his career, Alex promised himself he would only be staying at any one job temporarily—long enough to gain some experience before branching out on his own. But each time he considered leaving, he had been promoted and offered more money. With more money had come more toys, more trips, more expenses, and more debt. With so many financial obligations, he could no longer afford to leave his job. He certainly didn't have the savings to branch out on his own.

Early in his professional life he'd interviewed executives in their 40s and 50s about their job satisfaction. He found that half were very happy, but the other half were miserable. Alex observed a common thread in the interviews of the unhappy executives: at some point in time, after about a decade with a company, each one of them had given up. They had conceded that they weren't going to do any better financially than they were doing, and gave up on their dreams. In short, they settled.

Alex remembered this time in his life at his prior company. The company's vice president of executive sales was retiring, and he was the most successful of the eight sales managers at the time. Alex was the clear front-runner to replace the outgoing executive, but he also knew that this could be his time to make a break. His friend Tim had been urging Alex to start a business with him. They would be 50-50 partners and Alex could be the entrepreneur he had always dreamed of becoming.

Meanwhile, the allure of the new role beckoned. He could become the top sales executive in a company he already worked for. But Alex knew that with more money and more power came more responsibilities and more pressure, and that he'd be definitely earn every cent he made—the company would get their pound of flesh from him.

Although Alex was excellent at sales, he also yearned to develop his creative side, which was unchallenged in his current sales role. He yearned to manage a business from beginning to end, the way only an entrepreneur could do. But when it came down to it Alex couldn't make the move—it felt too risky. Alex chose to stay and assume the new executive role. Sadly, that position did not last long before the company went under, and he found himself without a job or an income. Meanwhile, Tim's new business was thriving.

Alex felt the loss of the missed opportunity, but now he was trying to face his failures without a heavy feeling of guilt or regret. No more justifying or rationalizing. No more feeling defensive. Later that evening, after he had returned from an uneventful day at work, he signed on to his first video conference with Victoria. He didn't know it yet, but the trap she had planned to discuss today was just as timely as her introduction to the first trap had been in Hawaii. It felt strange to sit in front of a computer to connect, compared to their previous side-by-side conversations; regardless, Alex felt eager to talk with Victoria again.

"It looks like we have a good connection, Alex. Can you hear me okay?" she asked.

"Loud and clear," he replied.

"Good!" she said with a smile. "Are you ready? Got that notebook out? I think you're really going to like this!"

"Lay it on me!" he laughed.

"The sixth trap centers around your passion for, and engagement with, your chosen profession."

"I'm not sure if *passion* is the word I would have chosen," Alex said, half-joking.

"I gathered that much. You are not alone, by the way. Today, more than ever, people settle for a career that doesn't motivate or inspire them. Their heart and mind are not engaged. They don't enjoy their work but they have become too financially dependent upon it to leave. Many people eventually find themselves engulfed in the sixth trap, which I call the Career Trap," Victoria explained. "Does this sound familiar?"

"To a T," Alex said. It was as if Victoria was reading his mind.

"Companies looking at levels of engagement in their employees have found rampant disengagement in the workplace. Why do you think this might be?"

"I can think of a lot of reasons," Alex replied.

"Well, I've read numerous studies on disengagement. It's not only a problem here in the United States but throughout the world. The outcome from all these studies reveals disengagement in the workplace at all levels. Companies are spending enormous amounts of money each year on this problem, but the problem still remains. In fact, in many situations it has only gotten worse."

"That's crazy, though at the same time, not terribly surprising." remarked Alex.

"Disengagement occurs when people don't find their work inspiring," said Victoria. "When people begin looking at their work *only* as a means to an end, when they say to themselves that they're only doing this job for a little while, till they find something better. But they get comfortable and eventually find themselves entrenched. They get a promotion, or a raise, or both. They get married, buy a house, or have a baby. Before they know it, they've become dependent upon that job and career because of their fixed expenditures or because of debt. They find themselves trapped, unable to leave their job and unhappy about their professional work.

"And then fear kicks in. Fear that if they change their career they will have to start all over again. Fear that they are too old to try something new. Fear that they will run out of money. Fear that they won't have the skills, education, or know-how to do what they really love. Have you ever felt this way?" asked Victoria, although she knew the answer would certainly be yes.

He sat up in his chair and met her gaze on the screen. "I've felt that way for years. I've always wanted to be an entrepreneur—to be my own boss. I have so many ideas and projects that I want to pursue. But in the meantime, I've become pretty good at my current job. I've developed the competency because I had to have the income, but my heart has never fully been in it. It's not the job I would choose now—I took it to provide for my family.

"My problem, as you know too well," Alex continued, "is that I have habitually lived beyond my means. When my income increased, so did my expenditures. Our home had to be upgraded—we needed it to be nicer and bigger. I financed more expensive cars. I bought the latest and greatest in technology. I had to have it all, and I had to have it right away. Let's just say that *delayed* gratification has not been my strong suit. The more debt I've taken on, the more entrenched and dependent upon my job I've become," Alex bemoaned. "I thought I was going after the American Dream, but quite frankly, it's become a nightmare."

He sighed deeply. "My biggest fear is *not* that I will fail or that I'm too old. My biggest fear is that I can't afford to leave my job. My financial obligations, fixed expenses, and debts are so high, I would have to declare bankruptcy if I lost my job and couldn't find another one quickly."

"That's a lot of pressure to live with, a real concern," Victoria empathized.

"It has been. But my world is changing, thanks to you. My debts are diminishing, and I'm finally starting to see my path forward to financial freedom."

"I can hear the excitement in your voice. Tell me more."

"I know people always say that the grass is greener on the other side, and I'm sure there are challenges and downsides to any new profession—but if I made the jump to do my own business, I would *finally* have the inspiration in my work life that I've been lacking."

"This move you want to make is a perfect segue to the ideas I want to share with you today," said Victoria. They are the three reasons why people settle and get stuck in their professional work. Would you like to hear more?"

"I'm all ears," Alex grinned.

"Okay: one, financial dependency on their job; two, their work environment is uninspiring; and three, they get in a career comfort zone," she summarized. "Let's address each of these separately."

Financial Dependency

"While most of us rely upon the income from our professional work to support us and our families, we need to avoid being too dependent upon it. The money we receive from our work is important, but it shouldn't ever become the main reason for working," Victoria said.

"When we become too financially dependent upon our job, the rest of our contributions suffer."

"What do you mean by 'our contributions suffer'?" Alex asked as he began to wonder about his efforts at work.

"I mean that when we become too dependent on a job, we start to become risk-averse and overcautious. We start to worry about how we might offend our boss if we offer ideas or suggestions that go against the company culture. And why do we do this? Because we are afraid to lose our job! We're afraid of sticking out, thinking differently, challenging others, arguing, or debating. And when we play it safe, our company isn't getting our best self. It gets our compliant self—the one that doesn't want to rock the boat or challenge the status quo—and that self is not the self we want to have at work."

"You see, the company that employs us expects us to bring our best self to work—our best thinking, ideas, perspective, approaches, suggestions, and efforts. When we decide to play it safe, we suffer and our company suffers along with us. This may be okay for a company if only a small percent of their employees are operating like this. But what if it's 30, 40, or 50 percent? Can you see how company productivity would suffer?" she questioned Alex.

"I can. My company is a prime example. I would say that, currently, 30 to 40 percent of the employees function that way. And I'll admit that I'm also a little more careful and cautious because if I lose my job, there goes my income, and any hope of getting out of debt. I can't afford for that to happen. Especially not right now." he said.

"You've made my point for me." Victoria smiled, ready to move on.

Uninspiring Work Environment

"Alex, it would be extremely unfair to say that the Career Trap is 100 percent self-inflicted by employees. The reality is that companies are culprits as well," Victoria continued.

"What do you mean?"

"I mean that many companies today are set up, structured, and aligned to bring out mediocrity in their employees," she answered.

"But why would companies do that?" Alex asked, bewildered.

"They don't intend to do it. If they're not careful, it just happens. As companies get bigger, they hire more managers, put in more structure, and create more rules and policies. There isn't anything intrinsically wrong with that—most companies need to cope with issues of growth. The problem arises because formal structure can curtail human innovation and creativity. People who take the initiative and are resourceful can be viewed as disruptive. Most companies don't have mechanisms in place to capture and channel employee ideas and suggestions.

"Oftentimes, employees will share approaches that run counter to the company's culture. Even though these ideas are more efficient and effective than the current way of doing things, they're often shot down and rejected. When creative employees see this happen a few times, they stop offering suggestions. If they believe their ideas won't be heard, let alone implemented or rewarded, why speak up? Sadly, this is the state of affairs for many companies. It's the reason why there is such massive disengagement," she explained.

"It doesn't make sense for it to be that way," said Alex. "But from my experience I have to agree, it's true."

Career Comfort Zone

"Alex, you'll relate to the third reason people succumb to the Career Trap. Like you, many people don't intend to stay in their job for the long haul. They make short-term decisions that often turn into long-term reality, and thus the abandonment of their professional dreams. Months turn into years and years can turn into decades. People find themselves spending their entire career at a job they didn't aspire to, but somehow they settled, got comfortable, and stayed."

"Yeah—my problem exactly," he chimed in. "Except I'm just halfway through my career, so there is still time for me to make a change," Alex said, hoping for Victoria's reassurance.

"That's right," Victoria smiled. "John Lennon once said, 'Life is what happens to you while you're busy making other plans.' And that is exactly how it goes. We look around, and before we know it, it's time to retire! We never intended to stay in that job. But there we are.

"You need to be very deliberate about what you do with your one beautiful life! Don't allow yourself be tossed about by the wind and the tide—unless of course you are on vacation in Hawaii." Victoria smiled. "Otherwise, that's no way to run your life, my friend."

Conventional Approach

"The conventional approach suggests that we should focus on what we love doing and everything will fall into place," Victoria continued. "The problem with this approach is that it only taps into one aspect of our life—what we are passionate about. It doesn't tap into our competencies. It may not challenge us and engage our minds. We might not be able to make enough money in this career to provide for our needs, much less wants. The passion aspect of our job is important, but provides too narrow a perspective if it's the only consideration. It doesn't take into account the other important dimensions of our life."

Epiphany Breakthrough

"Alex, there are four dimensions to a successful career—the financial dimension, the ideas dimension, the passion dimension, and the purpose dimension.

"When we have a job that engages all four dimensions, our entire self comes to work. The problem with a lot of professional work is that it only taps into one or two aspects of a successful career.

"A profession that pays me fairly or even generously for the work I do, but asks me to check my brain at the door or doesn't engage my heart, will not get the fruits of my best labors. Ultimately, I'll become miserable—frustrated by a stifled mind and a shackled heart! I'll feel stuck, and although my body may physically still be present, my mind, heart, and spirit will have checked out a long time ago.

"This happens to so many people," Victoria said dramatically, "but it doesn't have to be this way. Ultimately, you need to answer four questions about how your professional work relates to the four career dimensions: Am I well compensated financially? Are my ideas valued or used creatively? Am I passionately engaged? Do I have purpose or make a contribution?"

"No wonder I've been struggling with my current job situation. My passion and purpose have been totally left out of the equation!" Alex said.

"It sure sounds like it. Tapping into all four dimensions is critical for lasting fulfillment at work. When you can answer yes to all four questions, you and your profession are aligned. If you answer no to any of them, then you are likely to become disengaged."

"Well, I think I know how I'd answer . . ." Alex trailed off. "My current job is clearly misaligned. I couldn't quite put my finger on what was missing until now."

"This is the key to engagement and satisfaction in the workplace," Victoria pointed out. "If a company wants wholehearted engagement from its employees, it must attempt to satisfy all four dimensions of a successful career. Many professional leaders simply don't understand this. They think if they pay people well enough, they will have them for keeps, but that's rarely the case.

"Most people leave their company because of the way their boss treats them. In other words, they fire their boss. Often people leave a company because their work lacks passion, it feels mundane and lifeless. Sometimes, people aren't given autonomy to do what they deem best. It's as if companies foster an environment where feedback isn't welcome and new ideas are speedily squashed. In those cases, initiative is crushed. You've probably experienced that before, haven't you Alex?" she asked.

"Totally. It's a suffocating environment to work in, creatively speaking," Alex observed.

"Many companies haven't figured out how to unleash the potential within their employees. Companies that continue to operate like this will not be able to compete in the global marketplace in the long run. They will not survive because they are underutilizing the human ability to create and adapt," Victoria continued.

"This is exactly what happened to the company I worked for during the recession," Alex commented. "I used to just write it off as bad luck, but what you've described makes more sense."

"Can I make a suggestion?" Victoria interjected.

"Yes, of course."

"If you asked yourself these four questions on a quarterly basis and always sought to answer yourself honestly, you could avoid misalignment in work altogether. Do you think that's something you could realistically do?"

Alex reflected before responding. "I can definitely do that."

"Good man!" Her eyes sparkled as she spoke. "I love how Steve Jobs put it: 'We don't get a chance to do that many things, and every one should be really excellent. Because this is our life. Life is brief, and then you die, you know.'"[1]

Alex pondered the unsettling idea that time was running out. He sat in silence until Victoria took a deep breath and continued.

"Alex, the point is: your life is yours to live. You are the architect of your destiny. Will you choose a profession where all four career dimensions are respected and valued? Where your gifts and talents can be utilized and unleashed? Or will you continue to settle for less?" she implored.

"Well, like I said earlier, I do feel ready to make a change. I think I've been stagnant in my work life long enough!" He looked down at his learning journal to make sure he had captured all the points from Victoria's summary.

Trap 6: The Career Trap

Why?

1. We become financially dependent on our income.
2. Our work environment is uninspiring and doesn't engage our best self; thus we settle for a loss of passion and inspiration.
3. We settle into a career comfort zone as our short-term job turns into a long-term stay.

Conventional Approach

Do what you love and everything will work out in the end.

Epiphany Breakthrough

Do professional work that encompasses the four dimensions of a successful career: finances, ideas, passion, and purpose.

Alex read his notes aloud to Victoria. She didn't immediately respond. He drew his eyes from the journal to see her beaming with pride. "Alex, You're practically a certified trapologist already!"

PART

4 | Trap 7

Decision Day

It had been a couple months since Alex's last conversation with Victoria. He was alarmed to realize how frequently in the past he'd found himself playing out the Old-Alex narrative as it related to his work. Victoria had shared those insights when he needed them most.

It had been nearly nine months since Kim had separated from Alex. Since she had accepted his apology for his role in their breakup, the feeling had improved significantly between them. He felt a sense of hope that they could somehow, eventually, rebuild their relationship. But Kim seemed in no hurry to return to L.A. or their family. Her job in San Francisco was going amazingly well, and she loved it. She made a bimonthly trip to visit the kids, but she spent most of her time with them at her parents. Alex had only seen her in passing, always with other people around. At least there was a growing friendliness between them. He now viewed her in a new light, impressed by her self-sufficiency and competence. He realized that he had taken her for granted while they lived under the same roof. He vowed that, if given another chance, he would never let that happen again.

The holiday season was now in full swing. Alex wondered how he and Kim would share their children throughout the upcoming festivities. He missed Kim more than ever, and wondered if she ever felt lonely or thought about him as well. Funny little memories would randomly pop into his head: how she would tuck her long brown hair behind her ear whenever she was feeling shy; how she would play with her wedding band whenever she was having a thoughtful conversation; and how she'd throw her head back and laugh whenever he'd said something really funny. He loved to make her laugh. He had become weary of being the single parent, but he had to admit that his relationship with each of his children had improved dramatically in the past few months. Actually, it wasn't just that they had been on their own, Alex realized. That feeling of closeness was due to all the time and effort they had spent working together toward common goals.

Alex glanced across the kitchen to where the paper snake was taped to the wall. It had been shrinking consistently, month by month and was now barely as long as a yardstick. With disciplined spending habits, he and the kids had whittled it down to a third of its length. Even Kim had pitched in $2,000 a month to assist in their debt reduction efforts, as she considered it to be her debt, as well. Now, all of his credit cards had been paid off and cut into pieces. All that remained was the $18,000 Michael had so generously loaned him. In the next few months, with everyone's combined efforts, the snake would be gone—never to return. Now this was progress he could measure. If only relationships were as straightforward as debt elimination, he mused.

Alex realized if he were ever to get Kim back into their lives in a meaningful way, it would take similar focus and effort on his part. He would need to win her back, help her see what she was missing by being away. He hoped she would notice how much he'd achieved in her absence and appreciate the new story he was starting to write. He decided to call and ask her on a date when she came to town for the holidays to be with the kids.

He dialed her number before he could second guess himself and held the phone to his ear. As it rang, his heart started to race. Would she turn him down?

After six rings the phone went to voicemail and Alex left a message. Pretty anticlimactic. Now he would wait on pins and needles for her return call.

* * *

In the last few months, Alex had produced fantastic results for the company—the best in its entire history. He wasn't just efficient; he was exhibiting visionary leadership that caught the attention of his boss, his peers, and the office staff as a whole. But when he showed up to work on Friday, he sensed that something was going on in the office. Chaz was in an especially gregarious mood—like he knew something that Alex didn't.

The moment Alex sat down at his desk, the phone rang. His boss's boss, Rick, asked to see him. Alex wondered if something was amiss, given the strange way Chaz was acting. He stood up from his chair and walked into the hallway. Chaz, who was lounging just outside of Alex's office, watched him walk down the long hallway to Rick's office at the other end. Alex knocked lightly on the open door. Rick looked up from his computer.

"Hi Alex, come on it—take a seat. Can I get you a drink?" Rick offered.

"Hey. Yes, thank you. Water would be great."

"You've got it," he said as he tossed a bottle into Alex's hand.

Alex's curiosity got the best of him, and he jumped right in. "So what's going on? Anything I can do for you?"

"Well," Rick said, as his lips stretched into a big smile, "I have some good news for you. I'm pleased to offer you a new position.

We've been extremely impressed with your performance and leadership this year. So I'd like to promote you to be our newest Executive Vice President and a member of my executive team."

Alex couldn't believe what he was hearing. "Ahh, uhm . . ." he started to speak but didn't yet have the words. He laughed softly and began to rub the back of his neck with his hand. This was totally unexpected. Alex thought he would have learned about a restructuring of some kind or a new initiative. This new promotion came as an incredible surprise.

If he accepted the promotion, he could finally get back to where he used to be financially. He would be given the respect and compensation he felt he had earned and been denied all this time.

Yet Alex knew he was once again at a crossroads. As sweet as the offer was, he could see that it would lock him in for years.

Before Alex knew what he was saying, words began to tumble out of his mouth. "I can't take the offer, Rick," he said in a flurry. "And I can't work here anymore, either."

Alex saw his own expression of shock mirrored in Rick's face. "What? Are you kidding me? Why!" He flashed a look of surprise that quickly changed to displeasure.

"I don't even know what I'm saying. I didn't plan to do this. But I've wanted to start my own business for the last 20 years, and finally, I just have to go for it. I'm sorry." Alex didn't even recognize himself. His voice sounded like someone else's. He couldn't believe what he'd just done.

"Um . . . I'm completely stunned," Rick fumbled, trying to regroup. "Honestly, I don't even know what to say. Why the sudden change? You've been performing incredibly well. What are you going to do instead?"

"I don't know exactly what I'm going to do yet, but I'll tell you when I do. I just know I can't stay—I have to go for it."

"You don't even have a plan? That doesn't seem wise to me, Alex. Why don't you accept the offer and stay with us—at least until you know what you're doing. We'll make it worth your while," Rick pressed.

Alex pivoted for the door. He grabbed the handle, but turned back around. "I can't do that, Rick. I'm sorry. I have to say no." Alex thought for a moment. "I realize that this is a huge surprise, so if you'd like help interviewing for my position, I'd be happy to do so. And if you need me to hang around and train my new replacement for a couple of months, I'd be willing to help. Thank you for the opportunities you've provided me, Rick, but this is something I need to do for myself. I hope you can understand." Alex gave him a quick nod, opened the door, and walked out of the room. Rick was speechless, but he returned the nod.

Alex had barely closed the door to Rick's office when Chaz approached.

"Talk to me, man. Talk to me! Did you get the promo?"

"Yeah, I did," said Alex, still processing what had just happened. Chaz grinned gleefully. He clasped Alex's shoulder in congratulations.

"And you recommended me as your replacement, right?" he assumed with his usual air of entitlement.

"Actually, no. I didn't."

"What? Why? How could you stab me in the back like that?" Chaz's face contorted with confusion bordering on fury.

"I didn't stab you in the back, Chaz. I'm not taking the promotion. I'm leaving."

"What? Are you crazy?" Chaz scowled and threw his arms in the air. Alex took some strange pleasure in seeing his suave friend out of sorts. "I guess so," he shrugged, smiling calmly as he walked down the hall alone. He was finally free.

* * *

When Alex arrived home that evening, his daughter was at the kitchen table with her nose in a book. "Hey, Laura. What are you reading?" he asked casually.

"I'm preparing for the SAT," she replied.

"Come again?" said a shocked Alex.

"S-A-T, Dad!" she tried to hide the smile that spread across her face.

"Well, well, that makes me one pleased father," he smiled. Laura met his gaze with returned enthusiasm.

"So, who's making dinner tonight?" Laura asked.

"It's my turn," Alex said. He opened the freezer and emptied a large bag of frozen chicken nuggets onto a pan. He turned on the oven and slid the tray inside, then went to change in his bedroom. He was exhausted. Maybe he'd lie down, just for a moment. But he soon fell fast asleep. Forty minutes later, he was awakened by Michael's knocks on the door.

"Dad?" Alex stirred. *What was that terrible smell?* He propped himself up on an elbow as Michael popped his head into the room. "Dad, you left dinner in the oven. It's ruined now."

"Oh. Geez. Sorry, Michael. I decided to lie down for a minute and accidentally feel asleep. I guess I'll have to make something else."

"It's okay, old man. Mistakes are part of the process, right?" Michael teased as he slipped out and closed the door.

Alex blinked hard in an effort to wake up. Was he still dreaming or did his son just say that?

Just as Alex was thinking about what else he could make for dinner, his cell phone rang. It was Kim. His heart began to race. He hadn't realized how anxiously he'd been waiting for her return call.

"Kim," he said, answering on the second ring. "How are you?"

"Hi. I'm good. Everything is great. How are you? How's work going?"

"I'm doing all right," Alex said cautiously. He wondered if he should share the news from work. He knew Kim had supported his dream to become an entrepreneur, but she might not understand his decision to turn down the promotion. He hesitated for a moment, then decided to go for it.

"Actually, I had a pretty eventful day at work," he confessed.

"Oh really? What happened?"

"Well, I was offered a promotion to become an Executive Vice President."

"Wow, are you serious? Alex, that is such great news. Congratulations!" Kim said enthusiastically. "When do you start?"

"That's the thing . . . I don't. I turned the offer down," Alex replied, with nervousness in his voice.

"You what? You turned it down?" Kim gasped, hoping she had not understood Alex correctly.

"Yeah . . . I turned him down," Alex repeated.

The line went silent. "Alex, have you lost your mind?"

"Kim, wait . . ."

"Why did you do that?" she demanded. Alex could hear the anger in her voice.

"Kim, I'm going to start my own business. I'm leaving the company altogether once we find and train my replacement. I'm going to go for it. I'm finally going to go for it!" he repeated with enthusiasm.

"I can't believe what I'm hearing," Kim said, as her voice started to crack. "So, what on earth are you going to be doing for this business of yours?"

"I haven't figured that out yet. It'll come. You'll be the first to know when I do."

"I seriously can't believe you. You don't even know what you're going to do? And you are just going to walk away from not just your paycheck, but a promotion as well? How does that make any sense?" she petitioned.

"I know it sounds crazy. But I feel like the timing is now or never," Alex said with a measure of confidence.

"This is madness . . . completely irresponsible!" Kim fumed.

"Just say you support me," Alex pled.

"I can't do that. How could you ask that of me? This is downright crazy and irresponsible. I can't deal with this right now. I've got to go. We'll talk later," Kim said hurriedly.

"Kim, wait! . . ." he started speaking, but the line went dead.

She had already hung up.

Alex was deeply disappointed with Kim's reaction to the news. He realized it was a mistake to tell her so soon. He should have waited until he had some ideas up his sleeve. In a way, he understood where she was coming from. Kim had always been concerned with security. He could see why she thought he was acting irresponsibly, just as he had been with the purchase of the new convertible, but this was different. Couldn't she see that? Though his enthusiasm was significantly deflated, Alex still felt a sense of pride in his decision to start his own business. He'd have to figure it out along the way, but he hoped Kim would eventually come to understand his motives.

For as long as he could remember, Alex had wanted to start a business. He understood the timing for doing so wouldn't be perfect, but by cutting off all of his options he would be forced to figure out what his business would be. This certainly wasn't the most logical or practical way to conclude a career or start a business. But this was his way of doing things—spontaneous, emotional, and intuitive, with a tinge of crazy mixed in. Weren't many of the great entrepreneurs a little crazy for that matter?

* * *

The days went by and Alex found himself feeling anxious and uncreative. He couldn't think of the right idea for his business venture. After weeks of brainstorming, nothing seemed to click. He wondered if Kim was right. Maybe he'd acted rashly in turning down that promotion. Maybe he wasn't cut out to be an entrepreneur after all. Why couldn't he see the path ahead more clearly? At a particularly low point, Alex picked up the phone and dialed Victoria's number.

His words tumbled over each other in his rush to be heard and understood. After confessing his fears and insecurities, Alex was emotionally spent, feeling on the verge of failure.

"Alex," Victoria responded gently, "I'm proud of you. Taking a leap of faith to follow your dreams requires an immense amount of courage."

Alex deflected her support. "Kim thinks I'm crazy."

"She'll come around. Just wait and see," Victoria reassured. "She's supportive of you making the move eventually—just not in the way you wanted her to be right now. Frankly, a transition like the one you want to make in starting your own business is rarely a smooth one; it's more often traumatic and fraught with challenges. It will be a bit of an uphill climb, and that's once you figure out where it is you want to go! You are going to need to be patient with the process, my friend."

She waited for him to answer. Alex remained silent. He felt discouraged. Victoria prodded, "Do you have any ideas yet?"

"Not any good ones," he responded quickly.

"In these situations, I find the best thing to do is to listen to your heart. Don't force yourself to come up with a list of ideas. This isn't a mental exercise for the brain; it is an emotional exercise of the heart.

"Begin by asking yourself the following questions: What do you feel passionate about and excited by? What is life asking of you? What distinct contribution can you make that no other person on the planet can make in quite the same way?" Victoria encouraged him.

"I hear you, but I'm not used to operating that way. I've got to be practical; otherwise, I'll be stuck in the same place a month from now," he bemoaned.

"Not true," Victoria said. "I want you to try something for me, Alex."

"Okay . . ." he responded, not really wanting to hear what she had in mind.

"Over the next week, I want you to really ponder over this particular question: What does the world need from me that no one else can offer?

"And then I want you to be silent and listen to what your heart is telling you. Make a note of any thoughts that come to you. Can you do that for me during the next seven days?" Victoria asked.

"I guess so. Not your typical approach, but then nothing with you is typical," Alex conceded.

"No it is not! Call me back in a week when you've taken the time to pay attention to what your heart is trying to tell you," said Victoria.

"Okay," he said.

At first, Alex found this approach to be very awkward. It was very hard for him to shut down his monkey mind that was constantly moving from topic to topic. But as he became more mindful, he found that he had moments of absolute clarity—in the shower, while sweeping the kitchen floor, or on his morning run. Ideas started to build one upon the other, culminating in a eureka moment during his drive home on day five. In this moment, all the pieces came together, and he could envision where he wanted to go with his business venture. He couldn't wait another two days to share his idea with Victoria.

Alex picked up the phone and called Victoria.

"Hello Alex! Has it already been a week?" Victoria asked.

"No, just five days, but I couldn't wait another moment to share with you the idea I just landed on," Alex said excitedly.

"That's great! Let me hear it."

"Victoria, I want to set up a business that trains people how to become Trapologists," Alex spilled out. "I want to teach others how to escape the traps you've taught me about. It would be a survival training, of a different sort. What do you think? I think it could be huge!"

"Alex . . . I love it," Victoria enthused. "I can't think of a more inspired business idea than this. You are a fantastic example of overcoming each and every one of these traps. Your experiences will give people so much inspiration, hope, and courage," said Victoria.

"So you like the idea?"

"Like it? Why Alex, I *love* the idea. Why didn't I think of it first?" she teased. After a pause she added, "I have only two requests."

"Shoot," Alex responded.

"The first is that you do your initial kick-off program in Honolulu, and you give me the chance to be a participant in the program."

"Well, I thought that went without saying," Alex grinned. "As a matter of fact, I was hoping you would help me teach some of these traps since you are, after all, the original Master Trapologist," he laughed.

"I would be delighted to help however I can," Victoria responded. "My second request is that you allow me to become an angel investor in your new business."

Alex's jaw dropped. Then a huge smile spread across his face. "Are you serious? That is so generous—oh my—Victoria, I don't know what to say. That would be incredible!"

"I couldn't be happier about helping your business come to life, Alex!" Victoria beamed. "I also think we might have to officially give you the title of Trapologist. I think you've earned it."

"Well it's about time!" Alex laughed.

"Alex, let's talk more about this in a month. I've got to run to my yoga class right now. I also want to share with you the seventh trap. You didn't think we would end our sessions together with just six traps, did you?"

Alex shook his head, "What is it with the number seven?"

"It's simply a magical number."

Trap 7: The Purpose Trap

One month flew by and Alex's mind ran wild with thoughts of how to build his business. He couldn't wait to hear Victoria's perspective on everything he'd been thinking about. But he knew they wouldn't just dive right into the fun stuff like he wanted to. They still had another trap to discuss together, Trap 7. Alex didn't know if he wanted to hear it. He already felt like he was trying to change so much about himself all at once, and didn't feel like he could take on anything more.

He looked at the time and realized it was just past the hour they had set to reconnect. He picked up the phone and dialed her. Just when Alex thought it might go to voicemail, Victoria's voice cheerfully answered. "Hey there Alex, how goes the adventure?"

"It's going all right," Alex exhaled. "To be honest, I'm kind of anxious to learn what this seventh trap entails."

"Oh, don't worry about this one. You haven't even fallen into it yet, unlike all the other traps we've talked about previously. After we discuss this trap, let's talk about the business."

"How did you guess that's what I really want to talk about?" Alex joked.

"Because I'm a mind reader, Alex. It's time you knew the truth about me," Victoria joked back.

"Well, if that were true, it wouldn't surprise me in the least."

"Okay," she began, "As I was saying, the good news about this trap is that you haven't fallen into it yet. It's a universal trap that most people don't even realize exists, until they reach the end of their lives. They wonder why no ever said anything about it. You might call it the best kept secret in the world."

"You're killing me with anticipation," Alex sighed.

"Well, I've done a lot of deathbed research," Victoria continued.

"Of course you have," Alex noted and settled comfortably in his chair. "So what exactly does that mean?"

"It refers to studies focused on people who are dying (most of them older) and what they regard as most important in their life. You see, when you're on the verge of leaving this existence, everything becomes crystal clear—what may have seemed important earlier in your life completely disappears, and in its place your true priorities emerge."

"Makes sense . . . so what did they find was most important?"

"Relationships!" Victoria exclaimed so loudly Alex thought his phone's speaker would burst. He jerked the phone away from his ear and laughed as Victoria carried on excitedly.

"Your relationships and your experiences are the only things you take with you from this life. Everything else falls by the wayside: money, possessions, honors, accolades, properties, and toys. At the end, they are all meaningless. You can't take them with you.

"So I call this 'The Purpose Trap.' Its main characteristic is accumulation—the ultimate lie we don't discover until the end."

"The end, meaning the end of your life?" asked Alex.

"Yes. That's exactly what I mean. Except in your case, you will have discovered this truth in the middle of your life," she said. "That's why I'm so excited to share it with you.

"Listen, we've been seduced into this trap for a variety of reasons. After studying this topic for a long time, here are the top three reasons why.

"First, we are negatively influenced by an environment of consumption and excess. We see people with more material abundance than us and we begin to think that life is about accumulating. We are marketed to so heavily, with constant messages about all the things we need, that we unknowingly start to believe what we are hearing.

"Second, we believe that having that next new thing will make us happier than we are now. We are in constant pursuit of more and more stuff so we can finally be fulfilled and happy.

"Third, we view our possessions as a measuring stick for success. We consume competitively. He who has the most stuff wins. The more we have, the more successful we appear to be," Victoria summarized.

Although Victoria couldn't see him, Alex was nodding his head in agreement.

"Alex, are you there?"

"Yeah, sorry," he said, half startled. "I'm just listening . . . taking it in."

Accumulation Mentality

"I'll just keep going then. Please chime in whenever, okay?"

"I will," Alex reassured.

"Great. So as I was saying, it's so easy to get caught up in the race to accumulate, we begin to believe that accumulation is what life is all about.

"Years ago, Rob and I moved to Australia on a work assignment," Victoria said. The company couldn't afford to ship our household items by air—instead they would have to arrive by boat. Shipping by boat was two or three times less expensive, but it also would take two and a half months for everything to arrive, instead of two weeks by air," she elaborated.

"The company offered us a standard relocation package to cover the entire move, which included all of our current household items. However, if we brought less stuff with us, our move would cost less and we could keep whatever part of the allocation we didn't spend. So we had an incentive to bring less in order to retain some extra cash. I remember talking to Rob about what we should do. You know, when you're moving halfway across the world, you're really forced to answer tough questions like, 'Do I really need this?' and 'Can we do without this?' We decided to take only one-third of our belongings, as compared to what we took for prior work relocations within the United States.

"We eliminated what we could bear to part with at the time, and put the rest in storage to collect when we returned. But as we were away, we realized that we didn't miss one item that we had left behind. In fact, when we returned from Australia, we had forgotten about most of the things that had been sitting there for the past three years. After going through it, we decided to either give away or throw away most of it. We only retained about 10 percent of what we'd stored. We had lived fine in Australia without it, and we found we certainly didn't need it upon coming home. It felt so good to simplify and lighten our load.

"Rob and I decided that once a year we would go through our belongings as if we were moving again to Australia, and donate or discard all the unnecessary things we had accumulated. Our family has lived by the philosophy of *'experiences before possessions.'* Our move to Australia forever changed how we look at our possessions and, most importantly, helped us realize what matters most to us in life," Victoria concluded.

"Wow! Victoria, what a great experience. I really love the idea of assessing the worth and importance of our belongings every year," Alex said. "We've got a lot of stuff we could stand to get rid of, that's for sure. Probably half of what we have, or at least a third."

"Whether you keep one-half or one-third isn't the point. What's relevant is that you do an inventory check of your possessions at least every year to evaluate what's important and what you can let go of," Victoria clarified.

"There isn't anything wrong with possessions that serve a purpose," she continued. "But throughout our lives we tend to accumulate excess stuff that demands our attention. And that's a problem, because stuff tends to break down. We have to spend a lot of time maintaining and taking care of it. When we spend more time on stuff, we spend less time on the things that matter most. So, one way to spend more time with those we love is to consistently and systematically eliminate the excess stuff we accumulate."

"Yeah, that makes a lot of sense to me," Alex said.

Pursuit of Happiness

"Confusing purchases and accumulation with the pursuit of happiness is the second reason people fall into the Purpose Trap. People look at the wealth and prosperity of others who have more than they do and they assume they must be more content. These people suffer from the *if-only* syndrome. Here's some classic, all-too-familiar 'if-only' statements:

- If only I had that house, boat, cabin, toy, or gadget, then I would be happy.
- If only I was done with school and could start working, then I would be happy.
- If only I had a car like my neighbor's, then I could get a girlfriend and be happy.
- If only I had an extra $50,000, then I would be happy.

"Wait a second. What about my convertible?" Alex protested. "Before I turned it in, it legitimately made me happy. If Kim didn't hate it so much and if I weren't so tight on funds, I would have loved that car for a long time."

"Long time?" Victoria questioned. "I doubt that. The thrill of the car would have probably worn off in a year or two when you got your first dent or had to do a major repair. I'm not saying possessions don't bring you happiness; they can. It just doesn't last very long," Victoria explained.

"Yeah, I guess you're right," he admitted. "Throughout my life I've seen my enthusiasm for the latest gadget or toy drop off once a newer model arrives."

"That's my point. Happiness and joy, in the long run, come through relationships, experiences, and the knowledge we gain. These are the only things we can take with us when we die. Everything else we leave behind." Victoria reiterated. Sometimes Alex wondered if she had an open glimpse of the other side.

Competitive Consumption

"And now for the third and final reason why many people fall into the Purpose Trap. Success is defined in our society as if it were a competition, or a race to accumulate the best and the most. When you ask people how they define success you hear them talk about their job titles, their bank accounts, their net worth, their homes and cabins, their cars, or their art collection. Not to say that these things are bad in and of themselves," Victoria added. "They just need to be downgraded to the appropriate level of importance in our lives. More often than not, people don't define their own success by their marriage, their family, or their contributions. They may say those things are important, but their actions suggest otherwise.

"Instead, they have the order reversed," Victoria noted. "They are so caught up trying to impress each other with the possessions they have accumulated, the degrees they have earned, and the money they have stockpiled that they lose sight of the truly important things—character, service, contributions, family, and relationships.

"Unfortunately, so few people truly view success from this perspective. And that is why I call it the best-kept secret in the universe, because we often don't discover this truth until the end of life. It comes to us like a thunderbolt—we've been accumulating possessions while neglecting the critical things in our lives. And here's the biggest tragedy of all: once we realize that this is what life has been about all along, we've run out of time."

Alex thought about the sports car he had bought, recognizing it as the catalyst for Kim leaving him. It revealed so much about how he had chosen luxuries over his wife's feelings . . . how many years had he been doing that? Living as a married single. Putting his own wants before the needs of his wife and kids . . .

Alex's thoughts were interrupted by Victoria's voice saying, ". . . which leads me to share the epiphany breakthrough that will keep you from falling into this trap . . ."

Alex furrowed his brow and interjected, "But wait—what about the conventional approach?"

"Oh, good catch. I'm getting ahead of myself!"

Conventional Approach

"The conventional approach is to simply expand your capacity to keep and maintain all your belongings. Just think of it. Houses are cluttered to the brim, and garages are packed so full that many people can't even park their cars inside. On top of all that, we've seen a huge increase in the demand for storage units over the years. People are consuming at an alarming rate, and rather than carefully vetting what they own, they buy up more space to support their consumption," she sighed.

"Now that you bring it up, it really is astonishing," agreed Alex. "Just last week, on my way to work, I saw a new storage facility that seemed to have popped up overnight."

"I don't doubt it. This approach believes the answer to managing all of your stuff is to buy a bigger house," Victoria continued. "But if you can't afford that, then you should be able to afford a storage unit for only forty bucks a month, right?"

"I hear you," Alex added, "It's just a management system. It doesn't actually address the true issue of accumulation."

Epiphany Breakthrough

"That's right. The epiphany breakthrough, on the other hand, comes through realizing that true happiness does not come from possessions. It comes from serving others and making meaningful contributions that benefit other people long after we are gone. It is prioritizing experiences over possessions. It is living with the realization that bondage is not in owning things but in having things literally own you, from a time and maintenance standpoint.

"With this awareness in mind, sort through and simplify your possessions, asking if they are aligned with and serving your purpose.

It's not a question of whether something is useful or has monetary or status value, but rather, whether it's necessary and essential in furthering your priorities and goals.

"Alex, you will discover in life that epiphanies lie in the proper balance of things. I know a large extended family that owns a cabin on a lake in Idaho. This is definitely a possession that requires quite a lot of maintenance to keep it running, as well as a boat and related toys. But these particular possessions provide the opportunity for the numerous intergenerational members of this group to come together more often and build a strong family culture. Family members have come to cherish their time there together, and as a result, they are very close. This cabin is a possession with a purpose.

"Purpose. Meaning. Contribution. These are things that make us feel fulfilled and complete."

"There's a lot of truth in that," Alex agreed. "Everyone wants to feel like they're having an impact and moving toward their goals."

"Exactly. So why do we wait until the twilight years of our lives to realize this? Can't we see that happiness comes through the service we provide to our loved ones and others, rather than in accumulating more stuff?" Victoria queried.

"The deathbed research . . . that's a very powerful message," Alex mused.

"Isn't it?" she enthused. "Nobody on their deathbed ever wishes they had accumulated more stuff. What they talk about are the relationships, experiences, connections, and contributions they made. So, now that we know this, let's live life to its fullest and allow purpose to be the driving force in our life."

"Amen to that. I wholeheartedly agree," he expressed.

Like he had done with the last six traps, Alex had been taking notes throughout their discussion in his learning journal. Its pages were now full with the insights that had changed his life. He had come to cherish this journal and the growth represented there.

Trap 7: The Purpose Trap

Why?

1. We have an accumulation mentality: We are conditioned to believe that the purpose of life is to accumulate more stuff.
2. We are in continual pursuit of happiness. We believe that once we acquire the next thing, we will be happy.
3. We get caught up in competitive consumption: We view acquisitions as a measuring stick for success. Whoever has the most stuff wins! The more we have, the more successful we must be.

Conventional Approach

When your possessions outpace your capacity to hold them, simply add more storage space in your house and garage. If that is not possible, then you can rent a storage unit, or two or three.

Epiphany Breakthrough

True happiness comes from providing service, making meaningful contributions, and building lasting relationships. Possessions play a supporting role; they don't precede relationships in importance.

Victoria asked Alex, "Do you feel like a trapologist yet?"

"I'm getting there. I still feel like I have a long way to go."

"Well, thank goodness we still have time to continue living and learning," she smiled encouragingly. "And the journey doesn't end here! You and I have some work to do in our new training business!"

"Indeed we do. That seventh trap wasn't so bad after all, Victoria. I'm actually relieved to have it out in the open instead of letting my imagination run rampant. And yes, let's get on with planning our new business! The thought of it gives me hope and a renewed sense of purpose. I can't wait to dig in. Do you have some time to chat about it right now?

"You bet. It's about time we get to the fun stuff!" she exclaimed.

They spent the next hour throwing ideas around, talking as if they had been in business together for years. Their connection over the past year served to build their business relationship, giving them a foundation of trust and rapport. When they finally said goodbye, Victoria asked about Kim and the kids. Alex brushed it off with a hasty, "They're doing great."

"Well, please give them my best."

"Will do. Thanks, Victoria."

The Perfect Trip

Fast-forward two months. Alex had arrived in Honolulu for the kick-off program of his new business. He had scheduled the trip during his kids' spring break so they could come along as well. Since the business had launched, Laura had been working part-time while finishing up her senior year. Her role was to manage the logistics of the program. Michael came along for the sun and the surf. Fortunately, they arrived on the island a couple days early with plenty of time to prepare for the big event. Being back in Hawaii reminded Alex that one year had transpired since his separation with Kim. What a transformational year it had been. He hardly recognized himself and felt relieved to have the last 12 months behind him.

Because Alex was hosting the training program at the hotel, the family was upgraded to a beautiful two-bedroom suite overlooking the ocean. The turquoise water stretched out as far as the eye could see. Palm trees swayed gently in the breeze, and Alex found watching the waves roll in and out as mesmerizing as ever.

He started unpacking the clothes from his suitcase into a dresser drawer. Michael and Laura had dropped off their bags and raced each other to see who could get down to the pool the fastest. It was nice to have a quiet moment alone. With that thought, the phone rang. Startled, Alex picked it up and said hello.

"Hi!" Kim said brightly.

"Oh, hi Kim. What's up? Is everything okay?"

"Couldn't be better, actually. I just wanted to send you my best wishes for the program."

"Thank you. It's really nice of you to call. We're expecting a great turnout," Alex said optimistically.

"That's good news. How many people are coming?" she inquired.

"At last count I think we were at forty-eight."

"Well," Kim began cautiously. "I was wondering if there was any way you could fit in one more participant."

"Maybe. I'll have to check with Laura to see if we can swing an addition on such late notice. Who is it for?" Alex asked.

"Me!" Kim exclaimed.

"What? Are you serious? You want to fly out to Hawaii just to see the program?" Alex inquired.

"Well no, I mean yes, of course, but…Alex, I want to get back together." The words rushed out before Kim could pace herself.

Alex's heart began to pound. He must be imagining all of this.

"What was that?" he managed to squeak out.

"Didn't you hear what I just said?" she asked nervously.

"For a moment I thought I was daydreaming," he exhaled.

"Alex, I want us to be a family again."

Still stunned, Alex found himself without the words to respond. Kim continued. "I've been amazed by what the kids have told me about all the changes you've made. Michael's been telling me what a Florence Nightingale you've been around the house, and how supportive you've been of both of them and their interests. The whole debt snake thing is remarkable! I can hardly believe we are nearly out of credit card debt for good! I'm just so impressed. I never thought someone could change so dramatically for the better in such a short time. Well it doesn't feel like a short time. It's felt like ages . . ." she trailed off nervously.

Alex had thought the road to reconciliation with Kim would be long and arduous, and in some ways, it had been. Yet here she was, out of the blue, saying she wanted to come back? He was stunned.

Kim's words brought him out of his daze. "Most of all, I miss being with you. I've been so lonely without you."

Alex still didn't know how to respond. Kim's voice cracked with emotion. "Alex, I realize now how much I love you."

His eyes filled with tears. "Kim, I love you, too."

"That's all I needed to hear. Now will you open the door?"

"What?" He was confused.

"Open the door," she repeated.

"What door?"

"Alex, open the door to your room," she said firmly.

Alex dropped the phone and leapt to the door, throwing it wide open. There Kim stood, looking as beautiful as ever.

"Kim," he gasped, "I can't believe you're here!"

She fell into his arms, crying uncontrollably. They stood there for the longest time, neither willing to interrupt the moment. Finally she pulled back and looked up at her husband.

"I couldn't take it any longer," Kim explained. "I got on a plane without looking back."

"But what about your job? You love your job, Kim. You can't give that up," Alex reminded her.

"I know, I do," she assured as she wiped tears from her cheeks. "We haven't sorted out all the details yet, but I'm sure we can find a way to make it work." Alex pulled her close.

"Do the kids know you're here?"

"They have no idea," Kim looked up at him and grinned.

Just then they heard their kids' chattering voices coming down the hall.

"Hey you two!" Kim beamed, holding her arms open wide.

"Mom?!?" they both squealed simultaneously and raced across the room, nearly knocking her over with their enthusiastic embrace. Alex joined in the group hug and soon they were all laughing through their tears.

"Mom, what are you doing here? What's going on? Dad, are you in on this? Did you have any idea she was coming?" The questions tumbled out quicker than they could be answered.

Kim held them all close.

"How did I ever live without all of you for so long?"

They decided to order room service rather than go out for dinner that evening. The meal was surprisingly delicious and it was healing for all of them to be able to simply be together as a family after so many months of being apart.

Later that evening, Alex and Kim went for a walk along the beach. Alex marveled at how the simple act of holding hands could be so meaningful. They both enjoyed the feel of the soft sand underfoot and the gentle splash of the surf as the tide rolled in. Alex felt a deep sense of peace and gratitude. He knew he would never allow himself to take his wife or children for granted again.

* * *

Two days later, the day of the training program arrived. Everything was ready to go. The program would be one day in length with follow-up coaching sessions over the next seven months—one session per trap. Alex, Victoria, and Laura could hardly wait to see all of their hard work finally come to fruition. Kim couldn't help but marvel over the collective creativity that had brought this idea to life.

Initially, they had hoped to have about thirty participants. But by the time the enrollment period had closed, forty-eight people had signed up. They had even begun a waiting list for the next program.

An hour before the commencement, Laura was busy organizing the participant nametags. She paused when she read one of the names. She walked to where her parents and Victoria were standing.

"Dad, didn't you use to work and golf with a guy named Charles Mitchell?"

Alex glanced at the nametag. "What? No way . . ." he started. He turned to Victoria and Kim and exclaimed, "Chaz is one of the participants in our program! How insane is that?"

Kim rolled her eyes, and Victoria gave Alex a knowing wink. As the program was about to start, Chaz came strutting into the room. He had an orangey spray-on tan, a blindingly bright Aloha shirt, and his Ray-Bans perched on top of his head. He approached them and turned to the woman he assumed was Victoria with a cocky curiosity and said, "So, you're Victoria . . . the woman who turned Alex's world upside-down."

"In the flesh," Victoria replied with a gracious smile. "Why don't you take a seat next to my husband Rob and me?"

Kim and Alex had to smile as this exchange took place. Everything had come full circle.

As Alex looked out at the faces filling the room, he was overwhelmed with a feeling of immense gratitude. He stood before the group with a full heart, inspired by the possibilities ahead.

"Ladies and Gentlemen . . . Welcome to Trap Tales. The characters portrayed in this seminar are not fictional.

"In fact, you know them all too well. Just take a look in the mirror."

Trapologist Toolbox

Four Characteristics of a Trap

1. Seductive—A trap lures you in unknowingly.
2. Deceptive—Short-term gratification leads to long-term pain.
3. Sticky—Like quicksand, a trap is difficult to get out of once you fall into it. It requires an unconventional approach to get out and stay out.
4. Limiting—A trap holds you back from progressing towards your goals.

Four-Phase Progression: From Trapped to Thriving

1. Pain—The awful reality of the trap.
2. Recognition—The realization that you are stuck in a trap.
3. Success—The strategy you implement that enables you to get out of a trap.
4. Thriving—The progress you experience once you are free from a trap.

* * *

Trapology: The study of traps.

Trapologist: An expert at spotting and staying out of traps.

Epiphany breakthrough: The *epiphany* is the unconventional wisdom or insight that leads to a *breakthrough* in behavior.

Trap Inversion: Turning the trap upside-down by doing its opposite.

Traps 1–7 Overviews

Trap 1: The Relationship Trap—Operating as a Married Single

Core Reasons We Fall into This Trap:
1. We believe our upbringing is superior to that of our partner's.
2. We fail to shift our mindset from *me* to *we*.
3. We are unwilling to change, or we only agree to change if our partner changes first.

Epiphany Breakthrough: Create a shared vision for your relationship/marriage and agree upon a pathway to get there together.

Action Step: Write down and commit to memory your agreements with your partner.

1. How will we manage our finances?
2. If we have kids, how will we raise them?
3. What will be our roles in raising our family? Will we both work professionally? How will our household duties be divided and managed?

Trap Inversion: Whenever disagreements arise in your relationship, ask each other how important this issue is on a scale of

1 to 10 (where 1 is not important at all and 10 is extremely important). Be honest in your assessment. Allow your partner to have his/her way if they score higher on the scale than you on that particular disagreement.

Why is this a trap today?

- Half of the workforce is comprised of working women professionals.
- Can't rely on old ways of doing things—past cultural norms. We now need to negotiate different roles, especially housework.
- Separation and divorce have become a common reality.
- It's easier to meet new people online.
- It's easier to live separate lives; partners don't have to do things together.

The Relationship Trap Questions

1. In regard to my marriage/relationship, do we operate as a team or more like two single individuals?
2. Do we have a shared vision of the life we want to create together? What about the future excites us? What are we working toward?
3. In what ways did our upbringing differ? Where do those differences manifest themselves in our relationship? What are the biggest positives that we'd like to pass on to the next generation?
4. If we have children, what's our philosophy in raising them? How do our parenting philosophies differ? What can we do to become a more united and effective parenting team?
5. How will the household duties be divided? Do we both feel good about the arrangement? If not, what's our process for resolving the inequities?

Learning Journal

What insights have I gained from this trap?

What will be my next steps in applying these insights to my life?

Trap 2: The Money Trap—The Quicksand of Debt

Core Reasons We Fall into This Trap:

1. We have money myopia, which causes us to live in the now.
2. We fall into competitive consumption, and try to "keep up with the Joneses."
3. We are in denial, and believe that worst-case scenarios don't apply to us.

Epiphany Breakthrough: Make eliminating debt fun, interesting, and motivating by turning it into a game. Involve family members in creating a scoreboard to display in your home.

Action Step: Create your own Paper Debt Snake.

Note: The Paper Debt Snake represents only one way to do it. Be creative and make your own scoreboard representation that motivates you.

Trap Inversion: After eliminating your debt, direct all of the money that had been allocated to debt to building your own Green Paper Tree with three or four branches representing:

1. Cash savings
2. Investments
3. Education funds for your children if applicable
4. Retirement funds

Why is this a trap today?

- Easy access to credit.
- Unrelenting advertising and solicitation.
- Money is no longer physical and tangible—it doesn't seem real.

The Money Trap Questions

1. How will I visually track my financial progress? Could I create my own debt snake, or something similarly inspiring?
2. What can I eliminate from my life to better align with my financial goals? What changes do I need to make in my spending habits in order to get out of debt?
3. If I'm not in debt, what actions can I take to harness the power of compound interest?

Learning Journal

What insights have I gained from this trap?

What will be my next steps in applying these insights to my life?

Trap 3: The Focus Trap—Being Mired in the Thick of Thin Things

Core Reasons We Fall into This Trap:

1. We have too much coming at us—we don't filter what merits our energy, time, and attention.
2. We are perpetually connected to the Internet and the electronic world—most of this world consists of very thin things.
3. We lack patience and expect things to happen on our timeframe—immediately, if not sooner. We fail to recognize, or we forget, that the best things in life take time and are not instantaneous.

Epiphany Breakthrough: We can't do it all. We have to filter out the unimportant, detach from the minutiae, and learn to say "no" more often so that we can say "yes" to the things we value most.

Action Step: Do a quarterly check-in to determine whether you have been seduced by this trap and have gotten off target.

Trap Inversion: Plan a week or schedule a vacation where you completely unplug from the Internet, email, and the electronic world. How do you feel? How often do you want to do this?

Why is this a trap today?

- More is pulling at our attention than ever before. There is more to read, listen, watch, and do.
- Technology has been designed to pull at our attention, and make us compulsively respond to it. The brain gets a dopamine rush from completing a task in a game or getting a message from someone.
- Expectation of being always on and available, both professionally and socially.
- Computers/phones now have dual uses. They are a source for both work and entertainment, and the lines can get easily blurred and distractions may arise.
- Harder to distinguish between the important and unimportant in today's very noisy world.
- Unlimited amount of options and choices to entertain and distract us.

The Focus Trap Questions

1. Do I have a plan to eliminate the unimportant things in my life? How do I keep myself on track? How do I manage interruptions? How do I manage the inevitable crises that arise?
2. How much time do I spend in front of a screen each day? What percentage of that time is useful, and what percentage is trivial?
3. How do I get caught up in the thick of thin things? What is my biggest time waster? How could I eliminate or reduce its influence on my life?
4. How could I alter my work environment and schedule to spend less time on thin things? What bad habits or unnecessary meetings are getting in the way?

Learning Journal

What insights have I gained from this trap?

What will be my next steps in applying these insights to my life?

Trap 4: The Change Trap—Procrastination, the Killer of Growth and Transformation

Core Reasons We Fall into This Trap:

1. Change is difficult. It can be painful and uncomfortable.
2. We are tempted to postpone change for as long as we can.
3. As perfectionists, we live by the mantra: If I can't be perfect, I might as well not try.

Epiphany Breakthrough: Change courageously when my conscience dictates, instead of changing when circumstances force me to.

Action Step: When needing to make a pivotal decision, pause and reflect on what your conscience is telling you. Tap into this source throughout your life.

Trap Inversion: Stay ahead of the curve by having an educated conscience that operates as an internal compass throughout your life. Why is this a trap today?

- Easier to procrastinate with so much distraction pulling at us.
- Harder to distinguish between who we really are compared to how others see us.
- Why change when we can't be perfect? What's the point?

The Change Trap Questions

1. Have I thought deeply about the key changes I need to make in my life? What's keeping me from making these changes? What support systems (including family and friends) do I have in place to support me in making the necessary changes?
2. What changes have I been procrastinating? What circumstances or beliefs are holding me back from taking action? Can I be prompted to make changes due to force of conscience, or do I require the force of circumstance?

3. Do I exhibit perfectionist tendencies? If so, how does being a perfectionist limit me from making necessary changes in my life? What can I do to overcome these tendencies?

Learning Journal

What insights have I gained from this trap?

What will be my next steps in applying these insights to my life?

Trap 5: The Learning Trap—Mistakes, and Why We Got It All Wrong

Core Reasons We Fall into This Trap:

1. We don't take accountability for our choices. We hide our mistakes and rewrite our biographies instead of owning up to them.
2. We see our mistakes as character defects, rather than part of the learning journey.
3. We have a persona that we try to project to others. It becomes damaged and tainted when others see our flaws. We instinctively try to protect this image.

Epiphany Breakthrough: Rejoice and celebrate in the effort, the journey, and the process as much as in the end results. Mistakes are instructive. Learn from them instead of hiding them.

Action Step: Check in quarterly to see if you can answer these three questions in the affirmative:

1. When I make a mistake do I see it as a learning opportunity? If so, what have I learned?
2. Human beings grow through the formula of trial and error and multiple iterations. Do I consistently apply this same formula in my own life?
3. Many of the great innovations have come about through persistent effort and pushing through failures until a break-through is obtained (think of Thomas Edison and the light bulb). Do I apply this proven approach in my personal and professional life?

Trap Inversion: Encourage others to embrace their mistakes. Become a change catalyst in your family and organization. Exemplify someone who consistently lives and practices these principles.

Why is this a trap today?

- Rise of social media makes it appears that the lives of others are amazing and ours is boring and uneventful; therefore, I must have a persona that's better or different from what I truly am.
- Because everyone else looks perfect, I must hide or spin my mistakes and flaws from the view of others.

The Learning Trap Questions

1. Thinking about a recent mistake I've made, did I try to deny, justify, minimize, or hide it? Do I recognize when I am doing this? How can I embrace my next mistake as part of the pathway to progress?
2. Do I find myself dwelling on my past mistakes? Do I beat myself up over them? Have I learned to forgive myself? What's holding me back? When I'm experiencing difficult challenges, what kind of self-talk is most effective in helping me overcome them?
3. What can I do to help my family focus more on the effort and growth rather than the outcome? What can I do to help my team at work? How can I encourage others to embrace mistakes?

Learning Journal

What insights have I gained from this trap?

What will be my next steps in applying these insights to my life?

Trap 6: The Career Trap—Settling, or Losing the Passion and Inspiration in Your Professional Work

Core Reasons We Fall into This Trap:
1. We become financially dependent on our income.
2. Our work environment is uninspiring and doesn't engage our best self; thus we settle for a loss of passion and inspiration.
3. We settle into a career comfort zone as our short-term job turns into a long-term stay.

Epiphany Breakthrough: Do professional work that encompasses the four dimensions of a successful career—finances, ideas, passion, and purpose.

Action Step: Evaluate on a quarterly basis whether the four dimensions are being fully activated. This can be best determined by an affirmative answer to four questions:

1. Am I compensated fairly at work? (Financial)
2. Am I creatively utilized at work? (Ideas)
3. Am I passionately engaged at work? (Passion)
4. Am I making a contribution at work? (Purpose)

If you answer no to one or more of these questions, try to influence your work environment so that you can answer yes all of the time. If you can't answer yes after several quarterly assessments, consider working at a different company or starting a new profession.

Trap Inversion: Be a catalyst to help others at work to also find their passion and inspiration through this four-question assessment.

Why is this a trap today?

- We can find professional work that meets all four dimensions of a successful career.

- We shouldn't accept anything less than being fully engaged at work because so many options are available in today's marketplace.

The Career Trap Questions

1. Am I paid fairly for the work I perform? Why or why not? If I'm not paid fairly is it likely to change in the future? Why is my work being undervalued? Can I influence it? Or should I look for a job elsewhere where my work will be more valued?
2. Am I asked to check my brain at the door when I go to work? Do people ask for my perspective? Are my opinions heard and valued?
3. Does my company treat me with respect and dignity? Do I enjoy working with others on the job? How important are those work relationships to me? Do I feel like a valued employee, associate, and partner in the company? Do I have a mentor that supports and encourages me to be my best self?
4. How would I like to be remembered in my career? Am I proud to be associated with my company? What do I value most about my work? When I retire, will I be proud of my contributions?

Learning Journal

What insights have I gained from this trap?

What will be my next steps in applying these insights to my life?

Trap 7: The Purpose Trap—Accumulation, or the Ultimate Lie We Don't Discover until the End

Core Reasons Why We Fall into This Trap:

1. We have an accumulation mentality. We are conditioned to believe that the purpose of life is to accumulate more stuff.
2. We are in continual pursuit of happiness. We believe that once we acquire the next thing, we will be happy.
3. We get caught up in competitive consumption. We view acquisitions as a measuring stick for success. Whoever has the most stuff wins! The more we have, the more successful we must be.

Epiphany Breakthrough: True happiness comes from providing service, making meaningful contributions, and building lasting relationships. Possessions play a supporting role; they don't precede relationships in importance.

Action Step: Spend a day each year going through your belongings as if you were moving somewhere far away. Donate or discard what you have accumulated that is not adding value.

Trap Inversion: Repair a broken relationship or strengthen a weak relationship with someone you care about.

Why is this a trap today?

- We have more options than at any other time in human history—it is easier to accumulate stuff.
- Accumulation equals success, or at least that's what we are conditioned to believe.
- We live in a world of abundance; there is so much out there to acquire.
- Advertisers have become better and better at tapping into our emotions in order to convince us to accumulate more things.

The Purpose Trap Questions

1. If I was moving across the world, what would I bring with me? What would I leave behind? Could I eliminate any of these things from my life right now?
2. Thinking back on my recent purchases, which ones have really added value to my life? Which ones have not? What does this tell me about how I should make purchasing decisions in the future?
3. Who are the people that bring me the most joy? How much time do I spend with them?
4. What are some of my most treasured memories? What can I do to create more memories like those?

Learning Journal

What insights have I gained from this trap?

What will be my next steps in applying these insights to my life?

Acknowledgments

- To our wives, Pamelyn and Marie-Genet, who gave all their heart, passion, and spirit into this project. You truly transformed the book and your contributions are abundant throughout. Thank you for the endless edits you provided and for your inexhaustible enthusiasm and encouragement. We love you!
- To our families, for their love and support.
- To David Westley Covey, our most faithful, consistent contributor to the outline, structure, and ideas contained in this book. Thank you for guiding and supporting us, and for your boundless energy and positivity.
- To Jacquelyn Hayward, for streamlining and editing the minutiae from our manuscript and for adding color and perspective to Alex's story.
- To Jacob Covey, for researching and proposing the original seven candidate traps and for his helpful suggestions on the epiphany breakthroughs and trap questions.
- To Sara Avila Covey, for her masterful formatting and astute suggestions that helped the manuscript flow.
- To Joerg Schmitz, for his valuable contributions to the TrapTales methodology.
- To Wendy Gourley, Amy White, Carla Heesch, and Second Sight Studio for their insights, storytelling expertise, and energizing ideas, all of which brought Alex's story to life.
- To Maria Cole, for her positive affirmations, inspiration, and endlessly helpful edits.

- To Liz Gotter, our proactive and reliable assistant. Thank you for your support and suggestions.
- To our publisher, John Wiley & Sons, for their vision, direction, and support of this project. Specifically to Jeanenne Ray, Shannon Vargo, and Deborah Schindlar for their wisdom, expertise, and superb editing. We could not have done it without you. Thank you for making this process such a wonderful experience for us.
- To Stephen M. R. Covey for graciously agreeing to write the foreword and for being our present-day Victoria, who we both try to emulate in life.
- To all our business partners and friends across the world who make our professional lives so enriching and fulfilling. We value our partnerships with you.

Citations

Trap 1: The Relationship Trap

[1] Alan Deutschman, "Change or Die," *Fast Company*, May 1, 2005.

Trap 2: The Money Trap

[1] J. Reuben Clark, *Conference Report*, April 1938, 103.

Trap 3: The Focus Trap

[1] Kevin Matthies, "Mobile Social Networks Growing Rapidly, Says New Report," *Mobile Marketing Watch*, June 12, 2015.
[2] Nicholas Kardaras, "It's 'Digital Heroin': How Screens Turn Kids into Psychotic Junkies," *New York Post*, August 27, 2016.
[3] Steve Jobs, Interview with *BusinessWeek*, October 11, 2004.

Trap 4: The Change Trap

[1] Jim Taylor, "Business: Why Change Is So Hard and How to Make It Easier," *Psychology Today*, October 21, 2009.
[2] Ibid.
[3] Maxwell Maltz, *Psycho-Cybernetics* (New York: Simon & Schuster, 1960).

Trap 5: The Learning Trap

[1] Malcolm Gladwell, *Outliers: The Story of Success* (New York: Little Brown and Co., 2008), 50.
[2] Ibid.
[3] Carol Dweck, *Mindset: The New Psychology of Success* (New York: Random House, 2006), 175.
[4] Ibid., 176.
[5] Ibid., 41.
[6] Ibid., 37.
[7] Jim Loehr, *The Power of Story: Change Your Story, Change Your Destiny in Business and in Life* (New York: Free Press, 2007), 5.
[8] Ibid., 126–131.

Trap 6: The Career Trap

[1] Steve Jobs, Interview with *Fortune*, March 7, 2008.

About the Authors

David M. R. Covey   **Stephan M. Mardyks**

David M. R. Covey & **Stephan M. Mardyks** are widely seen as world-renowned experts in the field of Global Learning and Development. They are the cofounders and CEOs of SMCOV, Wisdom Destinations, and TrapTales; and cofounders and managing partners at ThomasLeland, Lead in English, and Streamline Certified. Past experiences include serving as joint COOs at FranklinCovey.

For more information about **TrapTales**, please visit their website at www.traptales.com, www.wisdomdestinations.com, or www.smcov.com.